DISCOVERING
YOUR
HEART

with the

FLAG
PAGE®

DISCOVERING
YOUR
HEART

with the

FLAG
PAGE®

A simple and powerful way to truly
understand yourself and others

Mark Gungor

DISCOVERING YOUR HEART with THE FLAG PAGE®
published by Laugh Your Way America! LLC

©2005, 2007, 2010, 2011 by Laugh Your Way America! LLC
International Standard Book Number: 978-1-935519-19-5
Mark Gungor, author

Unless otherwise indicated, Scripture quotations are from:
The Holy Bible, New International Version © 1973, 1984
by International Bible Society

Read This First

This book is intended to be used interactively with the colorful print-out that results from completing your Flag Page on the internet. We recommend that before you begin to read this book, you log onto www.flagpage.com take the assessment. In order to complete your Flag Page, you will need a code. Each person who takes the assessment will need their own code.

IF YOU ALREADY HAVE A CODE,

follow the instructions below to complete your Flag Page:

I. Go to www.flagpage.com

2. Click on, "Begin Your Flag".

3. When prompted, enter your code and fill out the requested information.

4. From here, you will be taken through a simple three step process. Be sure to complete each step before going on to the next as you cannot go back and edit previous pages.

5. When your Flag Page is completed, be sure to print it out on a color printer. This will allow you to get the most from your experience.

IF YOU HAVE NOT YET PURCHASED A CODE,

follow the instructions below to complete your Flag Page:

I. Go to www.flagpage.com

2. Click on "Buy Your Flag".

3. Follow the on screen instructions for purchasing Flag Page codes using a credit card. Once your transaction goes through, you will be in your new Flag Page Account and ready to go. Just click on one of your "available codes" and follow the directions to get started.

4. From here, you will be taken through a simple three step process. Be sure to complete each step before going on to the next as you cannot go back and edit previous pages.

5. When your Flag Page is completed, be sure to print it out on a color printer. This will allow you to get the most from your experience.

With your personalized Flag Page in hand, this book will come alive as Mark explains each part of your Flag Page to you in detail. If you have any questions or problems completing your Flag Page, please contact us at 866-525-2844.

Acknowledgements & Thanks

To my darling wife, Debbie, for her endless encouragement and support.

To Larry and Marsha Bilotta, whose brilliant insights into the motivations of people made the Flag Page possible.

To Diane Brierley, for her helpful contributions to the content of this book.

To Mary Ten Haken, for her careful review of these pages.

To Terry Kohler, for seeing the potential of this program.

And, finally, to my high school English teachers, who will be amazed that I've actually read a book, much less written one.

Table of Contents

Chapter 1
Who Am I?

"Before I formed you in the womb I knew you,
before you were born I set you apart..."
- Jeremiah 1:5

This is the basic question every human being struggles to answer. The answer is important because it helps us to determine our purpose, our reason for being.

The answer is difficult because we don't come with an instruction manual at birth telling us about ourselves, describing how we were wired and to what purpose our days should be dedicated. Even the simplest over-the-counter remedy comes with a label that describes what it is, what it should be used for and exactly how it should be used. When we come into the world, we show up naked and totally helpless. Ideally, we should be surrounded by the hopes, dreams and open honesty of our parents, grandparents, uncles, aunts, cousins and siblings. I believe this close family net was designed by God to act as a mirror for us, so that in the loving and supportive faces of our family we are able to catch glimpses of who we really are, what we truly look like and what we are capable of.

For thousands and thousands of years, human beings were surrounded by such an honest mirror. People would live their entire lives and die no more than a few miles from where they were born. Just looking out their front door they would be greeted by this network of involved family. Through the feedback and honest reflection of caring uncles or grandparents or cousins they could get a true sense of just who they were.

Sadly, since the industrial revolution, the Western world has witnessed the disintegration of this supportive family net. Today, family members are scattered all over the country. For most of us, the only glimpse we get of close family is during the holidays, as we rush in a seeming panic to spend just a few hours with this family member and that one. Yet even in those brief gatherings of siblings and parental units, we are able to catch quick glimpses of the "mirror", reflections of ourselves from people who know us better than anyone.

Truth be told, however, most of us hate the brutal honesty we are faced with in our families. It causes us to think "thank God we don't live near them the rest of the year", but we fail to realize that this uncomfortable network of family is our best shot at getting an honest picture of who we really are. This assumes, of course, that they are a healthy family, but that is becoming more and more rare. So many of today's families are made up of emotionally broken and dysfunctional people that it is unlikely they could provide much of a healthy mirror for anyone close to them anyway.

So where does that leave us? With millions of people who are unsure of themselves, not knowing who they are, why they are here or what they should be doing with their lives.

A person of faith has a great advantage over one who does not have faith. Through faith in God, these basic questions are answered. Who am I? I am a child of God. Why am I here? To bring glory and honor to the God who loves me. What should I be doing with my life? I should be living in such a way that my gifts and talents can minister to others and further God's kingdom. But even people of faith can struggle with the details. I know I am a child of God, but what kind of child am I? I know I should bring glory and honor to God, but how do I do that? I know I should be using my gifts and talents to further his kingdom, but what exactly should I be doing?

Enter the flag page. The flag page is a wonderful program that helps people discover who they really are at their best. It allows them the ability to truly discover their heart.

The flag page is different than many other personality assessments in that the focus is only on motivation -- what you truly love about life. The flag page is one of the few tests you will ever take that asks you no questions. Rather, you are asked to respond to 56 traits common to all people.

There are three simple steps:

Step 1

First, you are asked to choose as many traits as you honestly believe describe who you are. It is important that you do this from a general perspective, because most everyone CAN be any of these things. For example: Can I be "Low Key"? Sure I can. But does that generally describe who I am? Absolutely not! Therefore, I would not pick "Low Key".

If you are unsure of the meaning of a specific word, simply move the curser over the word and a simple definition will appear in the lower left corner.

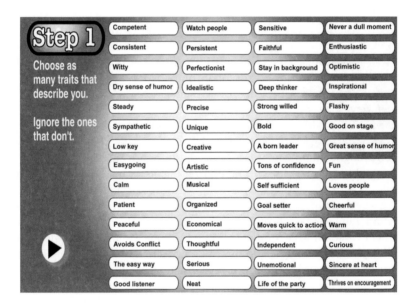

Step 2

Now, on a scale of 1 to 10, rate how good each of those traits makes you feel. A 10 means the trait makes you feel very good while a 1 means it just makes you feel "OK".

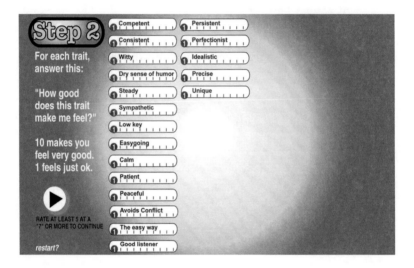

Step 3

Finally, you decide on the 5 traits that make you feel the very best -- in order of importance to you.

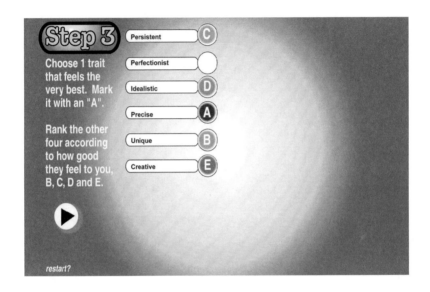

In seconds, the program calculates your input and creates your custom flag page. A single, colorful print out reveals...

1. Why you act the way you act
2. Why you re-act the way to do
3. What five things you need in your life to truly be happy
4. Where you are most likely to succeed in life

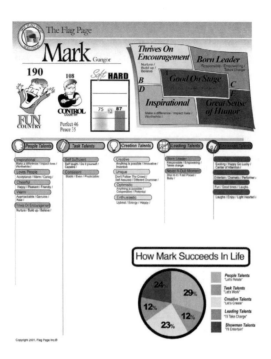

Appreciating the Differences

If you are doing the Flag Page as a couple, a common question that may arise when you see your Flag Pages is: "We don't have anything the same--is that bad?" The answer to that is NO! Since opposites attract, many couples will NOT have similar Flag Pages. The wonderful thing about the Flag Page is that it reveals to you just what those differences are and what they mean. Husbands and wives don't have to change the other person to be "just like me"! The goal is to understand your spouse and support his/her needs -- even if those needs are very different from yours. The Flag Page reveals a person's strengths, what is great about that person and what is truly in his or her heart. Couples can then learn to appreciate their differences and know they DON'T have to be just like each other to be happy!

People often think that if a couple has nearly identical Flag Pages then they make an ideal "match", but this is not necessarily true. Couples that have nearly identical flag pages can find themselves "competing" for the same motivations, and that can be a real source of conflict. For example: if they both have "Born Leader" on their Flag, this can create a struggle as they compete for that role. Successful marriages are not about having the same motivations. Happy marriages are created when couples learn to respect and meet each other's emotional needs--period. That can happen whether two people are very similar OR very different.

"I don't think my Flag Page® came out right..."

Let me try to give some possible explanations...

First of all, it is possible that a person filled out their Flag Page as they "wish" they were rather than as they actually are. This will result in a Flag Page that reflects desires rather than reality.

Secondly, it is possible that someone could over analyze the Flag Page, thinking "I guess I could be that..." The problem with that is anyone could be almost anything. One should only pick the traits they believe accurately and generally describes who they are.

A common question I hear from women is, "My husband's Flag Page did not come out right. Why is that?" When I ask why they think that their husband's Flag Page is wrong they'll say something like, "Well, his Flag Page says he is sensitive, but he's really a grump!"

You have to consider the possibility that the person truly did fill out their Flag Page correctly -- even if you don't usually see it. The best thing to do is ask them. If, for example, a person's Flag says they love to be Warm and Sensitive, but all you ever see is mean and hard, the problem may not be in the Flag. It could mean the person does not feel free to be who they really are -- so they become something very different. When a person feels forced to be something they are not, it usually isn't very good.

You need to trust your spouse when he or she agrees that their Flag Page is, in fact, accurate. Many women strongly disagree with what is on their husband's Flag Page. I know of women who feel so strongly about who their husband is that they do their Flag Page for them! Don't do that. Your husband needs to communicate what is important to him, not what you think he is or should be. You need to support that.

Where did the Flag Page® come from?

The developer of the Flag Page, Larry Bilotta, began developing the Flag in 1993. He closely examined personality tests such as the *Myers-Briggs* Type Indicator, True Colors, DISC and several other tests, as well as the ancient Hippocrates personality rating of Sanguine, Choleric, Melancholy and Phlegmatic. He found the strength of these tests was in the depth and detail of how they accurately portrayed what a person would act like in life. But, these test results told more than was necessary. The questions to complete the test could run into the hundreds and the multiple-page results were overwhelming. Due to the fact that these tests were created by psychologists and PhDs, the personality report summaries were complex and used words that only highly educated people seemed to grasp. Words such as "sensing", "intuitive", "dominant" and "analytical" are the language of the academic world.

In an attempt for a simpler approach, Larry picked a list of 56 character traits that described all four personalities while being careful to keep out any trait that seemed overly negative. He discovered that when people picked the traits they felt described them and then rated how strongly they felt about those traits, he could create an accurate printout of who that person was. Since their ratings were based on feeling and not thinking, it gave a clear picture of what drove and motivated people; it revealed what they truly needed in their lives to be happy and successful.

The Flag Page is NOT about personality, but rather, about motive. Personality is too big a subject for most people to understand or remember -- or for that matter, even care about. Instead, people desire to discover their best motives in order to create a map to see how they can succeed in life. The Flag Page is that map.

Chapter 2
The Four Countries

"What do you know that we do not know?
What insights do you have that we do not have?"
- Job 15:9

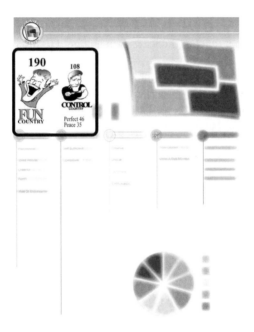

When you were filling out your flag page, you were unknowingly casting emotional votes for traits that belong to four distinct personality temperaments: CONTROL, FUN, PERFECT and PEACE. We refer to these four distinct and differing temperaments as "Countries". This is because they are very different from one another, just as different as people who come from different countries. Countries have different customs, traditions, ways of doing things, and words and phrases can have very different meanings.

Many years ago I was in Europe and had the opportunity to meet a young couple from England. They had a little boy who was a toddler and was just as cute as he could be. It didn't take long before I found myself playing some ad lib game with him as he ran about full of life and giggles. At some point I said to him, "Come here, you little bugger..." Suddenly, his parents shot to their feet and in a fit of displeasure, grabbed their little boy by the hand and stormed out of the room. I was pretty taken back. I asked another person who was with us, "What did I say?" In his proper British accent he replied, "Well, over here a 'bugger' is a homosexual."

I had meant no such insult! I tried to explain that to me, or back in the States, the word had no such meaning, but it did not matter. As far as these people where concerned, I had called into question the sexual orientation of the apple of their eye and they, despite my explanation, determined to remain offended.

That is what it is like when dealing with the four countries. We love the language and traditions of our own emotional Country and frequently misunderstand or become insulted by the others.

This stark difference is only exacerbated in marriage. Our differences attract us to each other. We sense that we could use the strengths that the other Country's resident displays. But then we get married and those very same differences drive us crazy. "If only you would be more like me!"

Marriage is not the only place where these differences show up. Parents from one emotional Country may not understand their child from another. The workplace often turns into a place of tension when these Countries fight for turf. And church members of differing emotional Countries condemn one another as they fight for what their emotional Country considers proper and fair. We are even quick to quote the appropriate scriptures needed to condemn each other: CONTROL people will refer to "being doers of the word", FUN people quote "rejoice in the Lord", PERFECT people prefer "be perfect, even as your father in heaven is perfect, and PEACE people are quick to point out that we should all get along and "love one another".

However, despite our best efforts to fight these differences, they will always remain. The answer is not to make others conform to your Country, but to be able to understand the language and customs of the other Countries and relate to those "foreigners" around you. It is only then that they stop feeling so "foreign".

In Florence Littauer's book, Your Personality Tree, she tells a story about her two grandsons who experienced the same event, but their "Countries" caused them to see the event in very different ways.

One night I called on the phone and Randy, Jr., said, "Have you heard the bad news? Ginger (their pet hamster) is dead. She died in her cage. I went to play with her and she was dead." He then delivered a fitting eulogy and gave me the details. In his (Perfect) way he told me how he and his father had found a little box in the garage, lined it with paper towels, wrapped poor Ginger in tissue paper, taken the box to a far corner of the back yard and buried her. "We had a funeral," he explained. "We'll always remember poor dead Ginger."

I was close to tears over his mournful musings of the memory of the hamster. When little Jonathan got on the phone, I said, sadly, "I hear Ginger died."

He replied, "Yup, she's dead all right."

"Did you have a nice funeral for her?" I asked, giving him an opportunity to share his version of the tragedy.

"No, we didn't have any funeral; we just dumped her in an old box with clowns on it, stuck her in a hole in the ground, threw some dirt over her, and that's the end of Ginger."

"Will you get a new one?" I asked.

"Well, we might get another one, but if that one dies too then it's bye-bye hamsters!"[1]

They both experienced the same event, but they saw that very same event in two completely different ways. Listening to one boy wanted to cause you to cry, while listening to the other wanted to make you to laugh. If you didn't know it was the same hamster, you would swear it was two different events. That is the power of these differing Country temperaments.

For our purposes, we will be focusing on your two highest scores. We call your highest score your HOME COUNTRY and your second highest score, your ADOPTED COUNTRY. The Adopted Country is a place where you still feel very comfortable and have the ability to understand parts of the language, customs and beliefs of that Country. The combinations of your home and adopted Countries can say a lot about you.

We call Control/Fun or Fun/Control people "The World's Greatest Leaders". They have fun, but they still get things done, and people like to follow them.

Fun/Peace or Peace/Fun people are referred to as "The World's Most Lovable People". And why not? These people love to have fun, and are able to easily get along with everyone. What's not to love?

Peace/Perfect or Perfect/Peace people (the largest group) are called "The World's Greatest Workers". They get along well with others, but are careful to get things right.

We call Control/Peace or Peace/Control people "The World's Best Owners/Managers". They get things done, but are careful of the feelings of others. This allows them to communicate well on a personal level while still keeping their "eye on the ball" of what needs to be accomplished.

Perfect/Control or Control/Perfect people (the smallest group) are considered "The World's Strongest Willed People". You better "get it done and get it done right!" These are the people who would be the happiest if they owned their own island country and had themselves installed as the ruling (albeit, benevolent) dictator.

Our final combination is Fun/Perfect or Perfect/Fun. We call these people "The World's Best Entertainers" or "Creative People". This is a unique combination in that it is a conflicted one. While all the other combinations flow easily with each other, this one is at war with itself. This is because Fun doesn't like Perfect and Perfect doesn't really care for Fun. Those who have this combination are usually quick to confess that they feel this inward struggle -- particularly if the scores of the two countries are very close. Those who don't understand these motivations within themselves often struggle as they swing from one Country to the other. When they are having Fun, they shoot Perfect in the head and can become slobs. When they are feeling Perfect, they can assassinate Fun and become mean and demanding. Those who have this combination need to learn that they can be both, and that they don't need to be at war with themselves. It is our hope that the flag page will help them to feel comfortable with who they are and just be who God made them to be.

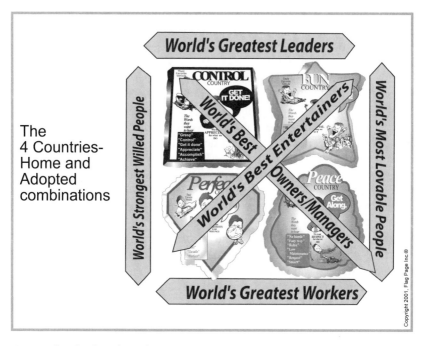

The 4 Countries- Home and Adopted combinations

As we take a look at these four temperaments, keep this in mind: it is not likely that you will be described with 100% accuracy. Every person is an individual, and we do not assume that everyone in the world can be perfectly summed up into four categories. If God can make billions of people and no two have the same fingerprint, I think it is safe to assume that God has created people with infinite varieties of temperament traits. I love the fact that the flag page takes this into consideration. While many other assessments simply categorize everyone into basic groups, the flag page shows how much you register in each group, as represented by the scores of each Country. We will discuss the scores later in this book in greater detail. For now, just realize that it is the combinations of all of these scores that show just who you are.

Having said that, there are a great deal of accurate generalizations that can be drawn from looking at your home and adopted Countries.

Let's take a closer look at these four Countries...

Chapter 3
Control Country

"But be ye doers of the word, and not hearers only..."
- James 1:22 (KJV)

Drive • Determination • Focus • Take Charge • Get It Done • Power • Serious

First, we have the rectangular shaped land of Control Country where everything is either black or white when it comes to the ways of Control people. Their number one cry: Get It Done! Their eyes can be steely and intense, their motions abrupt and they can put out some pretty strong vibes. Their voice can carry the sound of impatience and they are usually more interested in talking than listening. Their statements can come across as intense and their words can be quick, abrupt and to the point.

The shape of their land represents their hard and very direct ways. The people of Control Country share the belief that it is necessary to control their own environment. Their favorite vehicle is the bulldozer. They love to make a way where there is no way, while they move on to higher and greater accomplishments. The down side? They can sometimes plow over the people closest to them, and they are often totally oblivious to the fact they are doing it until the people around them cry out from their flattened position, "Hey, you're killing me!" The Control person may take notice, but will most likely respond "Yeah, but look at what I've accomplished!"

Jonathan often found himself being untruthful with his wife, Julie. Not big, nasty lies. Just little "omissions" and "creative re-enactments" of the truth that was starting to really frustrate her. Jonathan was so focused on keeping the bulldozer moving, he viewed explaining exactly what happened as an obstacle, so he simply put things in a most "convenient" way or told Julie what he thought she wanted to hear. He wasn't motivated to be a liar; he just wanted to keep plowing. After pointing this out to him on his Flag Page, it was easier for him to catch what he was doing. He learned that bulldozing the truth wasn't helping him. It was, in fact, slowing him down as Julie would confront him about his inaccuracies. He learned the best way to keep the bulldozer moving forward was to not create a situation that would require him to shut down in order to fight with Julie.

Pastor Johnson was a successful church builder. In fact, he could go to parts of the country where no one had ever succeeded with a big church and soon would have a congregation of over 1,000 members. He had a unique sense for doing whatever it took to get results. Somehow, he always knew who could help him reach his goals. His record of success would attract talented people who wanted to work with him. These people would give 100% of their energies to help Pastor Johnson succeed. Sadly, his staff members would soon notice that if they could help the pastor succeed, he would give them his time and attention; but if they had nothing specific to offer and just needed encouragement, Pastor Johnson had little to no time for them. As a result, the pastor found he had a continual problem of staff turn-over. His desire to "get it done" was so strong that others eventually felt "used" by him.

It is important for Control residents to remember that others are willing to allow them to ride their bulldozers to success -- just don't run them over! While these people desire to be appreciated, it can be pretty hard to appreciate someone after they have just gone over you with ten tons of bone-crushing steel.

We see in the previous graphic that when they are not driving the bulldozer, these people are conducting the orchestra; they are always in the lead and usually running things -- this is their favorite environment.

Look at the words they love to use and hear:
• Grasp
• Control
• Get it done
• Appreciate
• Accomplish
• Achieve

When you include these words in your message to them, they take great interest in what you're saying.

Control people's deepest need is to be appreciated for what they do. Everyone likes being appreciated for what they do, right? Yes, but this need goes much deeper for the residents of Control Country. They don't just "like" being appreciated, they MUST be appreciated. If they don't get the appreciation they so desperately need, they will become depressed and despondent and will begin to seek alternate ways to find appreciation. As we will see with all four of the Countries, it is this desperate search for what we truly desire that often gets us into trouble. A Control person may turn into a workaholic, since it is at work where he/she is most appreciated. A married Control person may find themselves drawn to an illicit sexual relationship because that other person "truly appreciates me".

Sadly, those closest to people from Control Country often fail to provide the appreciation they so desperately need. Why is that? Because everything about the Control person screams, "I don't need to be appreciated!" "I'm my own person." "I don't need anyone; I'll get it done myself if I have to." Now, they may or may not actually verbalize those sentiments, but the others around them hear them loud and clear. The wrong thing to do, however, is to deny these people what they need.

If you appreciate them, they become their very best:
• Born leader
• Tons of confidence
• Goal setter
• Independent
• Moves quick to action
• Bold

If they are denied the appreciation they need, they can become their worst:
• Bossy
• Impatient
• Quick tempered
• Demanding

- Know it all
- Arrogant

Control people don't always view the world like the residents of the other Countries. A Peace person and a Control person may both love people, but their underlying motivations can be very different. A Peace person may love people because he/she wants to make a difference in their lives. A Control person may love people because he/she needs them to reach their goals. The first may need people so he/she can inspire them while the second needs people so he/she can tell them what to do.

Often times, Control and Peace people marry one another. Their differences attract them to each other as they can sense that the strengths the other person has are what they need. Sadly, however, after the wedding cake has been eaten, they get frustrated with each other because "you're not like me!"

Control people can seem rather hard at times. But when you let them know you appreciate them and respect their accomplishments, the edge is softened. Clearly, life is better around a person from Control Country if the rest of us give them what they truly desire -- appreciation.

Control Country in Review

Control Country residents are all about: Getting it done.

Their greatest need: To be appreciated

Favorite vehicle: Bulldozer

Favorite environment: Conducting the orchestra, always in the lead and usually running things

Language: Grasp, get it done, appreciate, accomplish, achieve

Their voice: Impatient tone, talk but not listen, intense, quick words, abrupt and to the point

At their best: Born leader, tons of confidence, goal setter, independent, bold, quick to action

At their worst: Bossy, impatient, demanding, know it all, arrogant, quick tempered

Chapter 4
Fun Country

"Rejoice in the Lord always. I will say it again: Rejoice!"
- Philippians 4:4

Happy • Social • People • Mingle • Connect • Fun • Humor • Entertain

Next, we have my home: Fun Country. The star symbolizes Fun people's desire to perform and be the star of the show. Our battle cry is: Have Fun! The jet plane is our symbol for high speed and no limits. Unfortunately, we have been known to smash into brick walls from time to time. Others around us may ask, "Why were you going so fast?" "Why didn't you slow down when you saw the wall coming?" "Why do you take such stupid risks?" But no matter what reasonable question is posed to us, the answer is always the same, "Because it was fun!"

Fun people love to smile. In fact, we smile when we are talking on the phone, even though we know the other person can't see us. We find humor in virtually everything, even when it may seem odd or inappropriate.

Several years ago, my grandfather on my mother's side passed away. Though I never really knew him, I thought it would be the respectful thing to do, and I accompanied my mother back to Puerto Rico to attend the funeral.

During the wake, I sat back and watched the many uncles and aunts I never really knew (Wisconsin is quite a long haul from the Caribbean) and saw that they laughed and seemed to find humor in almost anything -- even at this sad occasion. Clearly, I come from a long line of Fun people.

After the service, the family carried the casket to the cemetery and when they arrived at the grave site, proceeded to lower my grandfather's box into the ground. As they tilted it downward in an attempt to put it into place, I noticed that they suddenly stopped. My Spanish is not very good (a result of being raised in Wisconsin), but I could tell by some of their comments that something was wrong. Soon I learned of their predicament: the casket top had popped open and poor old gramps had slid halfway out. I was shocked and appalled by what was happening but became even more shocked and appalled by the response from my mother and her siblings; they were struggling desperately to keep from bursting out laughing! In fact, the only one crying was a non-blood relative. I remember thinking to myself as I looked at these family faces, "No wonder I'm so nuts..."

Fun people can be very chatty and their big emotional highs are matched only by their big emotional lows. This, of course, can bring accusations that we are not very stable. We're stable alright; we're always looking for fun. We put out a vibe that says, "Everyone is welcome".

Notice the words Fun people love to use and hear:
• Really
• Happy
• Good time
• Funny
• Great
• Fun

When a Fun person feels validated and understood, they become their very best:
• Enthusiastic
• Optimistic
• Inspirational
• Great sense of humor
• Loves people
• Sincere at heart

When feeling misunderstood and invalidated, Fun people can become their worst:
• Talks too much
• Exaggerates

- Seems phony
- Forgets responsibility
- No discipline
- Easily distracted

The people in Fun Country tend to constantly be on the go in search of a good time. This, of course, can irritate the residents of the other Countries. "After all," they reason, "We understand about having fun, but can't you see there is a limit?"

The long answer to that question is: no.

Besides, why on earth would you want to limit fun? Fun is what gives life its thrill and energy, right? Not to the residents of Control, Perfect and Peace. Control, Perfect and Peace people tend to view Fun people as an oddity. "When we were children, we were like you too, but we grew up!"

Despite the encouragements (wet blankets, from Fun people's perspective) of others, Fun people are the eternal residents of Never Never Land. To us, Peter Pan isn't just a nice story -- it's a goal! Fun people have a strong need to be with other people because we don't like being alone. We enjoy visitors from the other three Countries and always welcome everyone. We want to be light hearted, likeable and we have a sense of humor about most things. All we ask is for you to give us approval for the way we act, that you notice us -- our strongest need in life. While many people like to be noticed, being noticed is a deep emotional need for the residents of Fun Country. In fact, if we go unnoticed, we can become depressed and despondent and (in the worst case scenario) can start "looking for love in all the wrong places".

Here is the catch: Fun people desperately need to be noticed. The problem is everyone else thinks they've been noticed enough -- so much so that they may actually go out of their way to deny them the attention they desire. They think that too much attention will "only encourage them" and, they're right. But that's the point: Fun people WANT to be encouraged by others. This can seem strange and odd to residents of the other countries.

Fun people love to be noticed -- even if it is for their blunders and mistakes. Many Fun people will openly share with others their most embarrassing moments or biggest, outrageous mistakes and failures. The residents of the other Countries sit in amazement that we can be so "open", "honest" or "self-deprecating". Actually, we are just wanting to be noticed. Notice us for our strengths, notice us for our weaknesses, notice us for our brilliance or notice us for our stupidity -- we don't care, just notice us!!

While I was working on this book, I had to fly into Cleveland, Ohio to do one of my Laugh Your Way to a Better Marriage seminars. As I was riding on the shuttle bus that took us to the car rentals, I could not help but overhear a woman as she was explaining to her husband why it took her nine hours to cross the small state of New Hampshire. She recalled in hilarious fashion how she and her girlfriend kept coming back to the same place -- for nine hours! Then, because it was so late, they checked into a hotel for the night. She told her husband how when they looked out their window, they saw the biggest, fullest moon they had ever seen. What made it even more spectacular was it did not seem to rise but held its glorious position all night long. When they walked out of the room the next morning, they noticed that what they had been seeing was a big street lamp!

By now, she had everyone within ear-shot laughing hysterically. It did not matter that a "normal" person would probably never admit to the stupidity of her trip. She was delighting her husband and the rest of us with her incredibly humiliating story and loving it the whole time. Why? She was a Fun woman who loved to be noticed.

Probably our greatest opposites are those from Perfect Country (we can drive them crazy and they can really get on our nerves). Perfect people love attention to detail -- Fun people hate it (just look at my desk). A Fun person can go to a mall, buy what they need, come back out and find that they have no idea where they parked the car. What's worse, they think it is hilarious. Residents of the other Countries (particularly Perfect) are mortified by such behavior.

"How could you forget where the car is?!"

"Why don't you pay attention?!!"

"What is the matter with you?!!!"

We, of course, think such responses are overly serious.

"Chill out!" would be our most likely response. Besides, there is no reason to "have a cow". After all, it will be "just fine". We then look forward to re-telling the embarrassing story to the first group of people we can find. Why? Because it is, well... funny! Besides, we enjoy the fact that you are laughing with us and noticing who we are. Fun people's greatest dread is that they will be ignored and go unnoticed.

When I present my marriage seminar, Laugh Your Way to a Better Marriage, I tell stories that people find hilarious. And they should -- they are very funny. Like the time I was arrested and strip-searched for drugs. (Care to guess where they looked?) If the same event had happened to a resident from another Country, it would not be a funny story at all. In fact, it could be a traumatic event that potentially could have left the person scarred for life. Pretty wild, huh? If it happens to me, it becomes a hilarious story that helps to underscore an important point that thousands of couples all across

America have benefited from. Have the same thing happen to a Perfect Country resident, and you have someone who may end up needing therapy. Amazing.

Fun Country in Review

Fun Country residents are all about: Having fun

Greatest need: Approval for the way they act

Favorite vehicle: Jet plane

Favorite environment: Being around people

Language: Really, happy, good time, funny, great

Their voice: Smiles on the phone, humor in everything, chatty, lots of lows and highs

At their best: Enthusiastic, optimistic, inspirational, great sense of humor, loves people, sincere

At their worst: Talks too much, exaggerates, phony, irresponsible, undisciplined, distractible

Chapter 5
Perfect Country

"Be perfect, therefore, as your heavenly Father is perfect."
- Matthew 5:48

Ideal • Exact • Precision • Feelings • Caring • Making a Difference

Next, we find the land of Perfect Country. Perfect Country's diamond shaped land represents these residents because they long for perfection with an inborn need to be precise and exact in all that they do. The train on the track is the vehicle of Perfect people because they want predictability and to know that they are going somewhere specific. If the rails are not exactly in the right place, the train cannot go forward. Perfect people are known for "stopping the train" if things aren't just right. As a result, they are frequently confused with Control people and often hear, "You are such a control freak!" They, however, do not desire control of their environment like the residents of Control Country. If fact, when you accuse a Control resident of being in control -- they usually smile and agree with you. When you accuse a Perfect resident of trying to be in control, they feel insulted. They are not trying to control things, rather, they desire that everything be right before proceeding. In Perfect Country, the residents can't stand it when things are wrong. They want to "get it right" under all circumstances. While Control people desire appreciation and Fun people want to be noticed, the residents of Perfect crave order and structure.

Because they so desire to get things right, they can use a lot of words to say very little. They worry if things are not just right and can remain serious and concerned as they hover over the details of life.

The cartoon of the magnifying glass shows how these people love to focus in on detail. They can make details "come alive" and as a result, are some of the most brilliantly creative people in the world. This is the land where the great artists, writers, poets, musicians, inventors, architects and technicians come from. They are very creative and sensitive people and will warmly accept you if you use the words they long to hear, because you are then speaking their language:
• Ideal
• Sensitive
• Right
• Feel
• Details
• Perfect

Of course, the magnifying glass also helps them to see what is wrong with, well... everything. That is most disconcerting to the residents of the other Countries. You see, when a Control, Fun or Peace person tell you what's wrong with you, they often mean it as an insult. But one of the ways a Perfect person shows their love and concern is to point out what is wrong. They think, "I love you, therefore let me tell you what is wrong with you." Of course, it does not feel like love to the residents of the other Countries, and they do not always appreciate it. Sometimes, even fellow Perfect Country residents may not appreciate it! But they do not mean it as an insult or a slam. In fact, if Perfect people did not care, they most likely would ignore you. But if they care, they often show it by telling you what you're doing wrong, where you are failing, or in what way you can improve on what you are trying to do.

They have a great desire for order and can place order as a priority over all other things. I often kid these people and tell them that if they had been on the *Titanic*, their greatest concern would have been that the furniture stay arranged on deck!

These are the people whose office, work space or home is always neatly arranged. Some people with very high Perfect scores (we'll talk about the scores a little later in this book) are the kind of people who iron and fold their underwear, have their shoes neatly sorted, all of their socks are laid out by color and style, and if you pulled open any drawer in their house, you would see everything perfectly arranged and in order.

Their environment can be very important to them. For some, just sitting in an empty room with nothing on the walls will create a sense of stress and tension in them.

Perfect people are probably the most misunderstood people in the world. Those without this motivation cannot understand what the big deal is and can fight them in their desire for order. You can imagine how a spouse, children, friends, or co-workers can easily mess with their need for order and neatness.

When a Perfect person feels validated and understood, they become their very best:
• Faithful
• Persistent
• Idealistic
• Creative
• Organized
• Thoughtful

Sadly, they are often misunderstood, are left feeling invalidated and can become their worst:
• Remember negatives
• Moody
• Feels guilty
• Too much time planning
• Standards too high
• Insecure around people
• Depressed

Perfect people can sometimes come across as tough and uncaring to others, due to their efforts to point out what is wrong and how things can become better. Others assume, therefore, that Perfect people can be handled in a rough way. They assume, "Hey, these people are always throwing darts -- I'll throw some right back at 'em, they can handle it!" But they can't. The secret truth of Perfect Country is that they are the most sensitive people in the world. Perfect people are always getting their feelings hurt by others. Because they feel things so deeply, they struggle to let these hurts go. Many spend years carrying around the slings and arrows thrown at them by others.

Forgiveness can be a real struggle for them -- not because they are hard-hearted, quite the contrary. They struggle because their hearts are so open and sensitive to begin with.

What happens to a Perfect person who is wounded too deeply? They become damaged. Then they take the perfection that they long for and turn it on themselves turning their desire for perfection into a deadly, self-inflicting weapon.

The breakdown of the family has been particularly damaging to the residents of Perfect Country. We estimate that nearly 50% of all residents of Perfect Country are in this painful category of what we call "damaged perfect". Parents who divorce or who are abusive or dysfunctional in any way, inflict great damage on Perfect children. In the same environment, Control kids just push their way past it, Fun kids try to dismiss it in as light a way as possible, and Peace kids make peace with their feelings. But Perfect kids take everything to heart, storing it all deeply in the vaults of their soul, hoping they can just keep everything locked away.

In his book The New Birth Order Book, Dr. Kevin Leman refers to these "damaged perfect" people as "discouraged perfectionists" and describes how many of them are committing "slow suicide". He writes:

> Your perfectionism will cause anxiety and whether anxiety is conscious or unconscious it's got to come out somewhere. Certain parts of your body will pay the price. That's why so many [discouraged perfectionists] wind up going to see psychologists and the first symptoms they notice are migraines, stomach disorders, or backaches. They are the worriers of life, the ones who develop colitis, ulcers, facial ticks, and cluster headaches.
>
> Some perfectionists function very efficiently, but underneath the polished, seemingly flawless exterior is usually a person who wonders how long he or she can stay ahead of the posse, continually frustrated, perhaps wondering, "Why do I do these compulsive things over and over?" Whatever your degree of perfectionism, I know it is a burden and certainly a source of stress. And I also know from working with hundreds of perfectionists that the answer lies in controlling your perfectionism and turning it in an entirely new direction.[1]

Dr. Leman has written two books designed to help those who have become "damaged perfect" - When Your Best Is Not Good Enough and Women Who Try Too Hard: Breaking the Pleaser Habits. I highly recommend these books to anyone who believes that their desire for Perfect has broken down, that the beautiful desire for creative and intuitive genius has been replaced by a self-destructive voice that tells them they are never good enough, that they can never measure up, and who are constantly haunted with the feeling that they must constantly try harder and harder, no matter how successful they are.

Perfect Country in Review

Perfect Country residents are all about: Getting it right.

Greatest need: Sensitivity to their feelings

Favorite vehicle: Train

Favorite environment: Closely examining the details of life

Language: Ideal, sensitive, right, feel, details

Their voice: Talks a lot to say a little, worries if it's not right, enjoys lots of little details, serious and concerned

At their best: Faithful, persistent, idealistic, creative, thoughtful, organized

At their worst: Remembers negatives, moody, depressed, guilty, standards too high, insecure

Chapter 6
Peace Country

"Let the peace of Christ rule in your hearts, since as
members of one body you were called to peace."
- Colossians 3:15

Harmony • Cooperation • Getting Along • No Conflict • No Disturbance • No Tension

Finally, we have the cloud shaped land of Peace Country – a land where you will find harmony and cooperation. Just as clouds move along at a leisurely pace, so do the residents of Peace Country. When war breaks out between the other Countries, Peace people quickly find a place to hide. When the bullets stop flying, they appear once again and quickly ally themselves with the winner. To these people, what truly matters is that we all get along.

When a Peace person feels validated and understood, they become

their very best:
- Competent
- Consistent
- Witty
- Patient
- Peaceful
- Good listener

When feeling misunderstood and invalidated, Peace people can become their worst:
- Fearful and worried
- Can't make decisions
- Too shy
- Little self motivation
- Resents being pushed
- Resists change

The gondola is their vehicle of choice, floating gently on calm waters -- swimming pools, if possible, since they don't like emotional waves. (Inevitably, these people wind up marrying someone who does belly flops in the pool!) Peace people believe that it is necessary for everyone to get along in order to obtain a stress free lifestyle without conflict.

If you listen closely, you will hear the land of Peace in their voices -- not a lot of lows or highs. They can be so laid back that they may not even acknowledge your comments. (This, of course, can really frustrate a Fun person, since their number one goal is that you acknowledge them.) Peace people are often very comfortable with long periods of silence during conversations. Why? Silence = Peace. These pauses can be very uncomfortable for the residents of the other Countries, but not to worry. These people just like to be in a state of calmness. Their calmness can seem to be a statement that they do not care or reflect their deep seriousness, but just when you think they are being serious, they will surprise you with a burst of unexpected humor.

The cartoon shows a resident of Peace country lying in a hammock while mowing the lawn. This is not laziness. It is a picture of efficiency to them because the people of Peace Country are all about low energy output while still getting work done.

They have very good social skills, since they are so willing to be cooperative. But being cooperative is where they run into problems because the residents of the other Countries are absolutely convinced that these people need what they have to offer. And since they are so "cooperative", they tend to be pushed about by one Country and then another.

Control residents say to them, "You know what you need? You need to be more productive!"

The compliant citizens of Peace Country politely agree.

Fun people come along, convinced that these people are in severe need of a caffeine fix, and offer to be their personal cheerleaders. "You need to be more excited about life! Come on; let's go have a good time."

Again, the Peace people are quick to agree.

"Your problem is you're not doing things right!" shout the holders of the Perfect passport. "Let me show you how you can be better."

Of course, the Peace people quietly comply. After all, who doesn't want to do things better?

Indeed, Peace people are great to get along with and can be pushed about rather easily. Easily, that is, until you cross the one line that Peace people will not tolerate. That is when you begin to insult them. For the Peace people's greatest cry is, "Respect me for who I am!" If they push too hard, Control people can make them feel stupid. Stretch them too far and Fun people can make them feel foolish. Admonish them too severely and Perfect people can make them feel worthless. It is crossing this line of personal insult, when you no longer respect who they are as individuals, that will cause Peace people to become upset and withdraw.

Julie found herself married to the man of her dreams. He was a take-charge kind of guy (Control Country) and his bold and confident ways were what attracted her to Jim. It did not take long, however, for Jim to notice that Julie just wasn't getting enough done every day. As a resident of Control Country, Jim felt it was his sworn duty to assist his Peace wife in the ways of Control.

At first, Julie was more than willing to learn. (Peace residents are always willing to do whatever they can to maintain the peace.) But Jim started pushing too hard and soon he began to make Julie feel "stupid". Suddenly, Julie began to resist. She became upset and no longer was interested in what Jim had to offer. She would cry at the simplest suggestion from him. Life became difficult, romance was becoming a distant memory, and the harder Jim tried to fix Julie, the worse things became.

Jim's mistake was that he crossed the line you cannot cross with Peace people -- you cannot disrespect who they are.

Peace people don't do well in conflict as you can see by their words in their language:
• No hassle
• Easy way
• Relax

- Low maintenance
- Respect
- Smart

Their deepest need is to gain respect for who they are…no questions asked. They will allow you to give input into their lives, just as long as you are careful not to insult them.

Peace Country in Review

Peace Country residents are all about: Getting along

Greatest need: Respect for who they are

Favorite vehicle: Gondola

Favorite environment: Calm and productive

Language: No hassle, easy way, relax, low maintenance, respect, smart

Their voice: No acknowledgements to your comments, long silence is comfortable, no highs or lows in voice, very serious-surprise humor

At their best: Competent, consistent, witty, patient, good listener

At their worst: Fearful, worried, shy, unmotivated, indecisive, resists change, can't be pushed

Summary of Countries

The importance of understanding these basic motivations cannot be understated. Without these insights, people tend to judge, criticize and condemn each other. Truth is we all love our own Countries but feel there is something fundamentally flawed with the others.

When visiting another Country or attempting to influence one of its citizens, it is always best to speak in the native tongue of that land. This can be challenging, since everyone desires to speak the language of their own Country. The Flag Page® is an effective tool in showing people how they can best relate to each other.

Here's an example: A fun wife hears about my Laugh Your Way to a Better Marriage® seminar. She is immediately hooked because of the title. She wants her Control husband to take her so she says to him, "Let's go! It will be fun. We'll have a blast!" But she is talking the language of her Country and she might as well be speaking Swahili to her Control husband. Better that she say something like, "I think we should go to that seminar. We will be able to learn some things that will result in better communication and allow us to achieve a higher level of success in our marriage."

Can you see the difference?

Finally, it is important that people stay true to their own Countries and *not* try to be like someone from another Country. When they try to be a resident of a foreign Country, they'll seem like an alien who doesn't fit in! A person who is not from Control Country, but tries to acts like a Control resident will, most likely, come across as mean. Someone who is not a Fun Country resident will seem phony and irritating. Imposters of Peace Country will appear apathetic and disconnected, while those pretending to belong to Perfect Country will act frustrated and depressed.

Many married couples wish their spouse would become more like them. Truth is, however, you don't really want them to defect to your Country -- they don't do it very well. It is better that they be who God made them to be. Besides, you were attracted to that other person's strengths for a reason; you need what they have to offer.

Chapter 7
Understanding the Scores

"Their measure is longer than the earth
and wider than the sea."
- Job 11:9

As I said earlier, it is not likely that any one person will *exactly* fit any of the four Countries that were just described. The Flag Page® system acknowledges that each person is a unique individual. It is when you look at the Flag Page® as a whole that one is able to get the most clear and accurate picture.

The scores of the four Countries are significant because they show just *how* intensely a person feels about each and every Country. For example, the higher the scores, the more *intensely* a person feels about who they are and the more likely they will display more energy than a person who has very low scores. An intense person will have very high scores and a very laid-back person will most likely have very low scores.

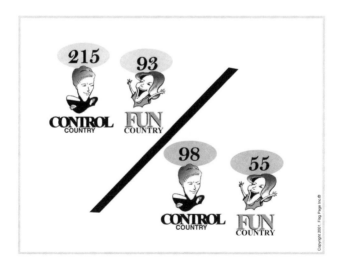

Any score over 100 means a person is becoming very expressive in who they are. You can see that the person who voted for 215 will feel much more intense about Control than the one who voted only 98. Unlike many other personality assessments that make all Control people the same or all Fun people the same, the Flag Page allows you to see much more detail about who you are.

In the previous graphic, you have two people whose results show that they are both Control/Fun. (Control being their Home Country with Fun as their Adopted Country.) While they may share much in common, the first person who voted 215 for Control and 93 for Fun is very different from the second person who voted 98 for Control and 55 for Fun. The numbers help to reveal your unique, individual heart.

The person with 215 for Control will more likely be as the person we described in chapter 3 than the person who only scored 98. Also, the difference between the scores will show how comfortable a person would be in moving from one Country to another.

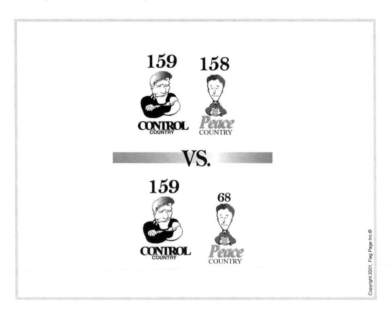

If a person votes 159 for their Home Country and 158 for their Adopted Country, that person can move much more quickly between the two than a person who would vote 159 for their Home Country and only 68 for their Adopted. The more "isolated" the Home Country's score, the more likely the person will be as we described in the Country chapters. What practical meaning does this have? Well, when a person has a much more isolated temperament, it is easier to understand and, perhaps, be able to anticipate how they will respond to a given situation. When an individual has scores that are very close, that person can move much more easily from one temperament to another and make it much more difficult for others to anticipate their feelings and responses. This can make it a greater challenge to work with such an individual, to have a son or daughter like this or, certainly, to be married to this type of individual. Don't misunderstand; this does not mean these people are flawed -- just different from those who are much easier to understand and predict.

What if a person scores very low in a particular Country? Well, if a person voted 0 for Perfect, you would have a person who would never make perfection a priority in their life. It doesn't mean they can't maintain order, it just means it is a very low priority for them. It also indicates how much understanding that person would have of someone from Perfect Country.

For instance, let's say a husband has a score of 159 in Control Country. Imagine his wife scored only 16 for Control. That means she is not going to have much of an understanding of the values and beliefs associated with her husband's Country and may have difficulty getting along with her Control husband until she gains the understanding of what Control Country is all about.

Perfect 52
Peace 0

In this example, we see a person who has a score of "0" for Peace. Does that mean the person can never be peaceful? Of course not. But it does mean that he or she is not likely to make "getting along" with people a high priority. A Peace person would start with the premise that, "We don't get people upset". Someone with a very low Peace score, however, may proceed with an attitude of, "Sometimes you have to get people upset. They'll get over it!"

Then there are those who score closely on all four Countries, making it possible for them to move from one to the other with a great deal of ease. These are the people who will find something to relate to in each of the previous chapters but don't think any one clearly describes them. This is due to the fact that they have the unique ability to become any of the four that they choose at any time of their choosing.

My wife, Debbie, is just such a person. All of her four Country scores are very close, and while the Flag Page program will assign her a Home and Adopted Country, in reality she can move easily around all four. There is no one single Country chapter that accurately describes her. In fact, even though I deal with the Flag Page every day and have seen thousands of couples experience their Flags, even though I teach on these truths all over America and even though I have written this book -- I still can't "peg" her in one Country or the other. Why is that? Because she doesn't really belong to just one. She has that wonderful gift of taking on the traits of whatever Country is needed in a given situation. She can shift at will and I'm never quite sure where she will be. On the other hand, the farther apart the scores, the less likely a person will be to make the emotional move from one Country to another, thereby making them a bit more easy to understand and, perhaps, easier to predict.

Chapter 8
Soft & Hard Motivations

"Consider therefore the kindness and sternness of God..."
- Romans 11:22

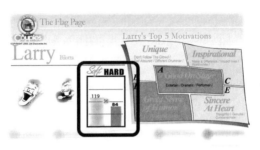

There is no greater single chasm in life than that between those who desire to be soft, relational and flexible and those who desire hard, to-the-point results.

We even see it in the church. There are those who only seem to see grace, mercy, and understanding. Then there are those who are more concerned about truth, righteousness, and upholding God's principles.

In his book, The Grace and Truth Paradox, author Randy Alcorn writes of the apparent struggle between grace and truth.

Truth-oriented Christians love studying Scripture and theology. But sometimes they're quick to judge and slow to forgive. They're strong on truth, weak on grace.

Grace-oriented Christians love forgiveness and freedom. But sometimes they neglect Bible study and see moral standards as "legalism."

They're strong on grace, weak on truth.

Countless mistakes in marriage, parenting, ministry, and other relationships are failures to balance grace and truth. Sometimes we neglect both. Often we choose one over the other.

Alcorn points out that Jesus was the perfect balance of grace and truth.

The apparent conflict that exists between grace and truth isn't because they're incompatible, but because we lack perspective to resolve their paradox. The two are interdependent. We should never approach truth except in a spirit of grace, or grace except in a spirit of truth. Jesus wasn't 50 percent grace, 50 percent truth, but 100 percent grace, 100 percent truth.[1]

Of the 56 motivational traits that people choose from when completing their Flag Page, some are considered very flexible and relational while others are considered very inflexible and results oriented. We call these traits SOFT MOTIVATIONS and HARD MOTIVATIONS. Notice that *both* sets of traits are good but just very different.

The 23 Soft & 23 Hard FLAG PAGE MOTIVATIONS

Soft	Hard
Sensitive	Neat
Sympathetic	Organized
Good Listener	Steady
Calm	Consistent
Patient	Unemotional
Peaceful	Serious
Low Key	Economical
Easy Going	Competent
The Easy Way	Independent
Avoids Conflict	Self Sufficient
Watch People	Idealistic
Warm	Perfectionist
Cheerful	Precise
Thoughtful	Goal Setter
Curious	Persistent
Thrives On Encouragement	Moves Quick To Action
Loves People	Life Of The Party
Witty	Never A Dull Moment
Dry Sense Of Humor	Flashy
Fun	Bold
Great Sense Of Humor	Tons Of Confidence
Sincere At Heart	Born Leader
Faithful	Strong Willed

Before I go further into the differences and significances of the Hard and Soft motivations, let's determine where you stand.

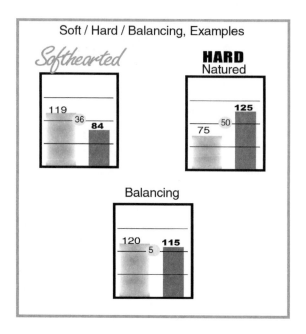

The Flag Page® measures how a person feels about the Hard vs. Soft traits in their life. The scores over the Hard and Soft graph show how intensely a person feels about those traits. The scores show where a person is most comfortable. What is of greatest interest here is the difference between the two traits (the number highlighted in the yellow circle).

When the high score moves more than 15 points in favor of the Soft, that person is referred to as a Softhearted person. We call them "relationship people". They are generally more patient and flexible. Because of their relational nature, Softhearted people are interested in feelings, are good listeners and need to use many words to express themselves. Due to their flexibility, they also tend to see the world in shades of gray. Black and white approaches seem overly harsh and unmerciful to them.

When the two scores are more than 15 votes apart in favor of the Hard, that person is referred to as a Hard Natured person. We call these "results people" – people who get things done. They are generally less patient and less flexible and see the world in black and white. To them, it is the truth that matters. Because of their results orientation, Hard Natured people just want the bottom line and prefer to talk and listen in bullet points. Hard Natured people often get a bad rap in churches. Soft people seem so much more "spiritual" because they are so quick to apply mercy and grace. But Hard Natured people are indeed wonderful and can be deeply spiritual. They know who they are, they are not as likely to be tossed "to and fro" by the winds and waves of uncertainty and can have a great deal of confidence about their faith. If the apostle James called "double minded" people "unstable in all their ways", then he had to have really liked Hard Natured people. They are not double minded about anything. They stay single focused on a task until it gets done. These are not the talkers of life, they are the "doers of the word" that James wrote about.

Softhearted people are quick to remind us that Jesus let people off the hook, that he said those who were without sin "should cast the first stone". True. But he was also the one who threw people out of church with a whip and the same one who called hypocrites a bunch of "snakes". As Randy Alcorn points out, Jesus was the perfect balance of grace and truth - what we call Soft and Hard. Bottom line? Both Soft and Hard people are valid and are important to building God's kingdom here on earth.

When a person's Hard and Soft scores are 15 votes or less apart, they are considered a "Balancing person". This doesn't mean that Soft and Hard people are "unbalanced". This simply means that these are the people who can more quickly and easily move between the Hard and Soft, tough and fair, grace and truth. Balancing people can relate well to both Soft and Hard people. They frequently find themselves becoming translators or arbitrators for the Hard and Soft people who don't understand each other. The challenge in dealing with Balancing people, however, is that Balancing people can change by the minute, choosing to be Soft and relational one moment and then suddenly becoming Hard and less flexible the next. While Soft and Hard people can be fairly predictable, Balancing people are much less so.

Again, take note of the scores; anything over 100 represents VERY strong feelings about these things. People with high scores tend to be very passionate and very intense. People with fairly low scores tend to be much less so.

The further apart the numbers are between the two scores of Hard and Soft, the more difficult it will be for that person to move from one to the other. People with a high difference in the Hard and Soft scores (50 or higher) tend to have a very difficult time when they feel forced to the "other side" and will generally be very uncomfortable or even over-react.

For example, a person with a difference of 75 to the Soft side will feel very uncomfortable if they feel forced to the Hard side. They will often over do it. These are the people who will "use a bomb to kill a fly". That is because they are so uncomfortable being hard and firm that they feel overwhelmed. They don't understand the world of Hard and often lack the appropriate skills that come naturally to Hard people. The same can be true of someone with a high Hard score and low Soft score. They will become very uncomfortable and awkward as they stumble about trying to be relational.

Soft Wants to be Emotional – Hard Wants to be Logical

Hard people desperately want Soft people to be Hard, but when Soft people try to be Hard, they don't do it very well. In fact, they are usually terrible at it. They tend to over-do it and can become mean and very harsh. Think: Incredible Hulk – "Don't make me angry, you won't like me when I'm angry." Bottom line, *Soft people make lousy Hard people.* They don't become logical people, they turn into "The Hulk".

Then you have Soft people desperately wanting Hard people to become Soft. The good news is that Hard people can indeed become emotional. The bad news is that they usually do it with a negative emotion. They too become "Hulk-like" turning into somebody you'd really rather not deal with. Bottom line, you don't want to force a Hard person to become emotional. *Hard people make lousy Soft people.*

Another movie analogy: Think of the original Star Trek series. Dr. McCoy represents the Soft and emotional. Mr. Spock represents the Hard and logical. McCoy and Spock always had a hard time getting along. Captain Kirk (think Balancing) would always step in between the two to make peace. Whenever McCoy would try to be logical and Spock would feign emotion, it was always awkward and funny. Neither one ever truly understood the other. And all of us who watched, always enjoyed it more when Spock was just being Spock and McCoy was just being McCoy. The moral of the story is this: Encourage and support people as they want to be on their Flag – remember, this is who they are at their best. Trying to get a person to be someone other than who they truly are usually ends with very disappointing results. Let Spock be Spock and McCoy be McCoy. And the rest of you Balancing people can continue to play the hero.

Another truth to be aware of: Hard people tend to translate life in terms of "right or wrong" while Soft people tend to translate life in terms of "friend or foe". This means that Hard people usually don't offend easily. If they don't agree with your input, they simply view it as incorrect and move on. If a Soft person, however, does not like your input, he/she will not take your input at face value, but assume that you just don't like them. As a result, you can be very direct with Hard people (in fact, they prefer it) but you should be a bit more thoughtful when dealing with Soft people.

Even though Hard and Soft traits are both good, make no mistake – predominantly Hard people have a difficult time relating to predominantly Soft people and vice-versa. Look at the following chart:

Let's call ZONE 1 "When everything is going great", ZONE 3 "When everything is going wrong", and ZONE 2 "The transition zone".

Notice that whether everything is going great or everything is going wrong, the Hard and Soft people *never* feel the same!

Soft Attitude Scale

ZONE 1
1 Faithful
2 Sincere At Heart
3 Thoughtful
4 Cheerful
5 Good Listener
6 Warm

ZONE 2
7 Patient
8 Unresponsive
9 Insecure

ZONE 3
10 Self Pity
11 Thoughtless
12 Touchy
13 Resentful
14 Dishonest
15 Defensive
16 Jealous
17 Critical
18 Two Faced
19 Manipulative
20 Back Stabbing

HARD Attitude Scale

ZONE 1
1 Considerate
2 Quiet Strength
3 Firm
4 Decisive
5 Goal Driven
6 Tough but Fair

ZONE 2
7 Strong Willed
8 Opinionated
9 Impatient

ZONE 3
10 Insensitive
11 Know It All
12 Abrupt
13 Cold
14 Sarcastic
15 Intense
16 Demanding
17 Forceful
18 Mean
19 Cruel
20 Abusive

This scale can also be used to show the "At Their Best" and "At Their Worst" sides of Softhearted and Hard Natured people, similar to that of the four Countries. When a person is being validated and understood and their needs are being met, they will live up in ZONE 1, at their best. When they are not being understood, if their needs are not being met and they are not feeling supported for who they are, they will descend down the scale to ZONE 3 and become their worst. We refer to ZONE 3 as the danger zone. It's easy to see why! People cannot live in this kind of environment continuously without wanting to seek out some sort of relief valve. It may come in the form of lashing out or, in the case of a married couple, divorce may seem like a realistic solution to their problem.

The Flag Page® helps us to see the emotional needs of people. If those needs are respected and met, that person will become their best and move into ZONE 1 and stay away from ZONE 3.

Review

SOFT people are relational.
HARD people are results oriented.
SOFT people are more flexible.
HARD people are less flexible.
SOFT people see the world in many shades of grey.
HARD people see the world in black and white.
SOFT people need many words to express themselves.
HARD people speak in bullet points.
SOFT people tend to view input in terms of friend or foe.
HARD people tend to view input in terms of right or wrong.

Chapter 9
The Flag - What You Need in Your Life to Truly Feel Happy

"...I will let you go and will tell you all that is in your heart."
- I Samuel 9:19

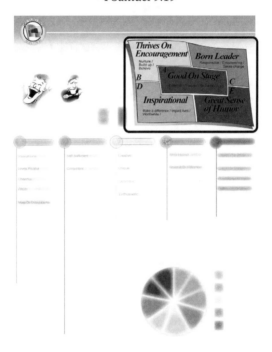

Now we come to the part that gave the Flag Page® its name – the five motivations that print out like a "Flag". These are the top five motivations of your life listed in order of importance to you. This is the "picture" or "photograph" of a person's heart that I mentioned at the beginning. Consider this; of the 56 traits that were presented to you when you first did your Flag Page, you chose to turn down 51 and to select these five. This represents who you are at heart. If a person has these five desires supported in their life, it brings them joy and fulfillment. If these five motivations are not supported, or worse, are criticized in their life, that person will struggle to feel happy and fulfilled.

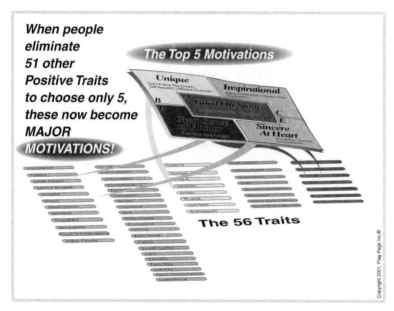

Acknowledging and supporting the Flags of people around you will create an atmosphere where people will rise to be their best, resulting in a win for all. When these Flag motivations are not met, people feel more insecure and are less willing and able to try to meet the needs of others' Flags. So by attempting to nurture and support the natural motivations of other people, you increase the likelihood of getting your own needs met.

Look at the five motivations on your Flag. These words represent the very core of who you are, the things you desire the most about life, the key to your happiness and the road map to your success.

Your Definitions

The first step to understanding and appreciating your Flag is to define exactly what those words mean to you. In the appendix of this book, you will find definitions and explanations about each and every trait that appears in the Flag. I suggest you turn there, read what it says so you can have a starting point, but then come back and write your own personal definition of what each motivation means to you on the next page.

For You

A motivation _____

Your definition:

B motivation _____

Your definition:

C motivation_____

Your definition:

D motivation _____

Your definition:

E motivation_____

Your definition:

For Your Spouse

A motivation _____

Your definition:

B motivation _____

Your definition:

C motivation_____

Your definition:

D motivation _____

Your definition:

E motivation_____

Your definition:

It is your own definition of what each of the boxes in your Flag means to you that is the most important.

Your Rules

After you have defined your top five Flag motivations, the next step is to create your Rules. A person's Rules Flag is the action tool of the Flag Page. To help you understand what a Rules Flag is and how to create it, here is an illustration:

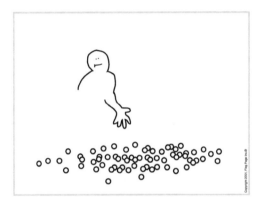

When you go online and complete your Flag Page, it's as if you threw 56 marbles containing positive traits on the ground and said to yourself, "Now pick up only five trait marbles that you really love." You sort through the marbles, eliminate 51 of them and now hold a precious 5 in your hand.

"Great!" you say, "but what do these five traits really mean to me personally?" You think about it and then write five definitions that interpret what the five trait marbles mean to you.

Now, in order for people to support you, they have to know exactly what to do and what not do so they never offend these five meanings. For that, we need to turn your meanings into Rules. Rules are clear statements that people either do or do not do. For instance, a Rule may say, "Accept my help and act on my advice." Now everyone knows clearly what you want.

Because your personal "Five Rules" come out of this process, you now have the ultimate communication tool: Your five most critical Rules, deep from the heart of who you are.

To Create a Rules Flag

Now we want to find the Rule behind the meaning of each motivation. What is the need you have in your meaning statement? What can someone do to support that need? Your Rule can be either negative or positive. Negative: "Don't try to get out of commitments you've made to me." Positive: "Keep your promises to me under all circumstances."

Example: Let's say a person has "LOVES PEOPLE" in the A box of their Flag. Their meaning statement may be: "I love to interact with others". Their Rule may be: "Understand my need to be with people". This would become their #1 Rule to feel loved. And so on for the other four motivations.

Now, write down each motivation and your corresponding Rule.

For You

A motivation _____

Rule:

B motivation _____

Rule:

C motivation _____

Rule:

D motivation _____

Rule:

E motivation _____

Rule:

For Your Spouse

A motivation _____

Rule:

B motivation _____

Rule:

C motivation _____

Rule:

D motivation _____

Rule:

E motivation _____

Rule:

Your motivations are the greatest needs you have in life and your Rules show your spouse or others what they need to know in order to support your Flag.

Teenagers find this process to be particularly helpful. No other group has a more difficult time expressing who they are and what they need, than teenagers. The Flag Page has proven to be a powerful tool in helping young people discover who they are and clearly communicate to the adults in their life what they need most from them.

Personal Mission Statement

Here is a final exercise for you to do. Take just the themes in those five motivations, and create a single sentence that becomes your personal "Mission Statement". This may sound like a simple thing to do, but some can find it rather challenging. You may find it helpful by first writing a sentence or two about each individual motivation.

Look at my Flag Page motivations:
A motivation: Good on Stage
B motivation: Thrives on Encouragement
C motivation: A Born Leader
D motivation: Inspirational
E motivation: Great Sense of Humor

From this, I created my personal mission statement:
"I thrive on the encouragement I receive from being in front of people as I use humor to lead and inspire their lives."

It took me a while to come up with that, but it felt really good when I could boil down my Flag to a simple statement.

Why is it important to create your own mission statement? Because once you write it, it causes you to ask the question, "Am I fulfilling my mission?" Sadly, many are not.

When I first experienced the Flag Page®, I was working as an associate pastor for Bayside Christian Fellowship in Green Bay, Wisconsin. My duties included working with the music department and overseeing the church's video production department. I was hired because I was a skilled piano player and had years of experience running my own music and video production company. I had won numerous local, regional, national and international awards for excellence. In short: I was very good at what I did.

For my whole life, all I heard was that it was important to do what I was good at doing. Unfortunately, I was struggling inside, at times fending off mild feelings of depression.

One day Arni Jacobson, the senior pastor, had all of us do our Flag Pages. To tell you the truth, I thought it was really stupid. I hate doing "personality assessments". When I heard that the Flag Page® was such a simple test, I was relieved. Many assessment profiles can ask you 200+ questions. When I saw just how simple it was, I sneered, "How can they tell anything from this?"

When I saw my Flag Page printout, I was stunned. There, before my eyes on a single, colorful printout, the desires of my heart lay for all to see. I remember lighting up as I saw the smiling face of Fun Country and as I read the words in my Flag: Good on Stage, Thrives on Encouragement, A Born Leader, Inspirational and Great Sense of Humor. Then, suddenly, I felt downhearted. The person explaining my Flag to me asked, "What's wrong?"

"All of these things in my Flag..."

"Yes?"

"Well... that is my problem."

"What do you mean?"

"Well, I want to be in front of people and be the leader, and that's wrong."

"Who told you that?"

I started to think back over the previous 20 years. Years of pastors telling me that wanting to "be in front" was sinful pride and wanting to be "the leader" was stubborn rebellion. I had squashed the very motives of my heart, motives that God put in me, dismissed them as faults and sins, not as gifts and strengths. Since I was good at music and video, (talents that just happened to serve those pastors) I was encouraged to just do that.

I eventually wrote out my mission statement. It was clear after doing so that I was not doing what was truly in my heart to do. Pastor Arni was the first guy to encourage me to start being who I really was meant to be. With his help, I launched my Laugh Your Way to a Better Marriage® seminar and started pastoring my own church. Needless to say, the Flag Page® has had a dramatic impact on my life.

How the Top Five Motivations Influence the Home Country

Let's look at your Home Country. Each of the four Countries has its own set of characteristics that come with being a "resident" of that Country. Remember that the higher the scores associated with the person's Home and

Adopted Countries, the more intensely he feels about those characteristics. People live and act according to these four value systems, but it is also important to consider what influence the **Top Five Flag Motivations** have on how people live through their Home Country.

As an example, people with Peace as their Home Country are generally less tolerant of change which is disrupting to their need for peace, routine and stability. BUT, if a person chooses Easy Going and The Easy Way as Motivations in his Flag, chances are he will react differently to change than a Peace person who places Consistent and Steady in his Flag. The Easy Going/Easy Way Peace person will not fight or resist change openly because of his need for no conflict and a life that flows around obstacles. Force a change on him or her and you may not hear a complaint. The Peace person who puts Consistent and Steady in his Flag is saying, "I want this non-changing condition to exist and anything that threatens this Consistent and Steady condition makes me very uncomfortable."

Here is another example of how Flag motivations influence a person's Home Country. Person A: Home Country of Control, with Flag motivations of Fun, Creative and Moves Quick to Action vs. Person B: Also Home Country of Control, but with Flag motivations of Strong Willed, Born Leader and Self Sufficient. Control country resident "A" is not as intense, not as in need of making results happen as Control Country resident "B". The "A" resident is less intense, more interested in people (Fun), and moves at a quick pace to solve problems with a creative solution.

Flag motivations may intensify or tame certain characteristics of the four Countries. It is very important that you look at what is in the Flag and consider the way those Motivations contribute to and influence how you are most likely to succeed in life.

The Colors of the Flag

The Flag Page uses only five colors. The colors are connected directly to the Five Talent Families shown below the Flag—discussion of this area to follow. Each of the 56 Traits belongs in one of the Talent Families. When a trait makes the Flag itself and becomes a motivation, it carries the color of the Talent Family with it. This way it is easy to see at a glance that a Flag filled with five blue motivations is saying that this person is highly motivated to be working with people. On the other hand, a Flag with four green task motivations shows a major passion for hands-on work. The yellow is creative, orange leadership, and red represents the showman talents where humor and entertainment are strongest.

Emotional Security Checkpoints--The Five Motivations That Help People Filter Their Lives

There are five motivations that act as "filters" for people. We call them the Emotional Security Group:

• Self Sufficient
• Independent
• Faithful
• Sincere at heart
• Competent

These Emotional Security Checkpoints work just like an airport security system where you are guilty until proven innocent. That's why airport security checks are so uncomfortable for Americans. Until you have been thoroughly "checked out" by Homeland Security, you are considered "dangerous". People with any of the five filtering motivations in their Flag screen people entering their world. They have a process by which they establish the level of safety or threat posed by others. By running people through their own filtering questions, they can find out just how safe a particular person is and what level of threat that person might pose for them.

• **Self Sufficient** and **Independent** cause the person to look at those on the outside trying to enter their world and asks the question **Do I REALLY need you?**
• **Faithful** wants to know **Can I trust you?**
• **Sincere at Heart** probes to find out **Are you genuine and are you fair?**
• **Competent** asks **Are you good enough?**

The more of these filtering motivations in the Flag, the tighter the Emotional Security System is, the more screening will take place. Your first question then becomes, "Is this a good thing or a bad thing?" Answer? It's a good thing for that person. Remember, this is what they love, what they were programmed for right back to their childhood and it turns out that in most cases, these are what their father or mother valued. If the Flag represents what they love, then these individuals with these traits love to filter people. It makes them feel safer. If you allow them to do this and accept that they always will, then you have a much better chance of having these people accept you as one who understands and accepts them as they are. Often, these filtering people are criticized for trying to filter others. Don't do that. Do what you can to accept that these filters bring them their own quality of life that puts a limit on how many people can enter their "inner circle". (It is interesting to note that in a study of six thousand people who completed their Flag Pages, these five filtering motivations are the most commonly found in Flags.)

Matched Sets

You should also be aware of what we call "Matched Sets". When both motivations appear on a person's Flag, it is like an exclamation point. These people *really* feel strongly about these traits.

MATCHED SETS
• Precise + Perfectionist
• Organized + Neat
• Self Sufficient + Independent
• Consistent + Steady
• Unemotional + Serious
• Artistic + Creative
• Idealistic + Optimistic
• Witty + Dry Sense of Humor
• Good Listener + Watch People

Conflicting Motivations

Sometimes, conflicting motivations can appear in a person's Flag. For example, if a person has both "Good on Stage" and "Stays in the Background", they should explore why that exists. It may be a simple case of clearing up the definitions, or it may be a sign of confusion in their life -- the result of some kind of trauma in the person's past. In this example, they may love to actively be in front of people, but were made to feel badly about it and told that they should live quietly in the background. It can help for the person to talk through any seemingly conflicting motivations so they can feel free to be who they really desire to be while giving themselves permission *not* to be whom they have felt forced to be.

Here's a list of some conflicting motivations:

- Fun / Perfectionist
- Low Key / Life Of The Party
- Witty / Serious
- Tons Of Confidence / Thrives on Encouragement
- Avoids Conflict / Bold
- Unemotional / Life Of The Party
- Calm / Life Of The Party
- Avoids Conflict / Strong Willed
- Stays In The Background / Good On Stage
- Patient / Moves Quick To Action
- Unemotional / Warm
- Easy Going / Bold
- Born Leader / Stays In The Background
- Serious / Great Sense Of Humor

Chapter 10
The Talents

"Whatever you do, work at it with all your heart..."
- Colossians 3:23

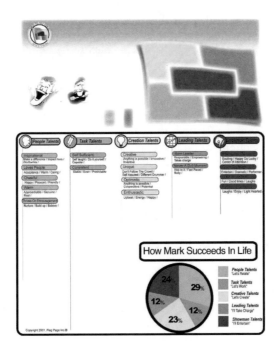

Finally, we come to the list of Talents on the Flag Page.

These are broken down into five categories:
1. People Talents – *"Let's Relate"*
2. Task Talents – *"Let's Work"*
3. Creative Talents – *"Let's Create"*
4. Leading Talents – *"I'll Lead"*
5. Showman Talents – *"I'll Entertain"*

The traits that appear here are the ones that you rated at least a nine or ten. These are the Talents that most influence and inspire you. (You may find it helpful to discuss what some of these words mean to you. Remember, you rated these nine or ten, that means they are very important to you.)

IMPORTANT: it is critically important to note that these are things that a person *loves* – not what they are able to do. For example, a person may be a competent leader, yet show little or no leading talents. While that person *can* lead, the Flag Page reveals that they don't necessarily *love* to lead. Remember, the Flag Page is about revealing what a person truly loves about life.

Some people will only have the motivations that appear on their Flag showing up under the talents, while others will have many additional motivations appear. Any motivation that appears in addition to their Flag motivations simply shows other things that you feel very strongly about.

Often, couples are interested in seeing how many traits they have that are the same. Some couples have a lot of matching traits (we consider five or more a lot) while others have none. What does this mean? Simply this: Couples who have a lot of matching traits will be different from those who don't have any -- that's all. It doesn't really mean anything. A successful marriage is not about two people having "a lot in common". It's about people who respect and support what the other loves and needs in his or her life, period.

Also, you may want to take notice of how many Talents appear in the Talents list. More than 25 is a lot. This may simply mean a person is very passionate about life or may represent a person who is struggling to become everything to everyone and can have a difficult time concentrating in just one area.

When people vote for the 56 traits, their highest votes -- the 9s and 10s, remain in the Talent Family list which creates the visual pie graph. The pie chart allows you to instantly see where a person's core foundation interests lay by looking at your two largest Talents...People, Task, Creative, Leading or Showman.

Chapter 11
Summary

"Blessed is the man who finds wisdom,
the man who gains understanding..."
- Proverbs 3:13

Empire State Building Analogy

To help you see that the Flag Page® is a full story that sums up a person's deepest motivations, imagine each of the four parts of the Flag Page® as if they were different parts of an entire building...the Empire State Building.

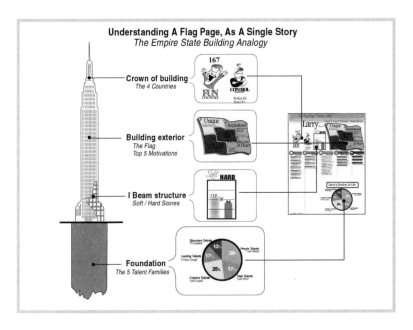

The foundation of this New York City landmark is represented by the Five Talent Family combinations. Talent Families are the foundation because they are underground, supporting the whole building. They are not easy to see, not even for the person them self. When people vote for the 56 traits, their highest votes, their 9's and 10's remain in the Talent Family lists which create a visual pie graph. The pie sections allow you to instantly see where a person's core foundation interests lay...People, Task, Creative, Leading or Showman.

Next, look at the I-beams that hold the building together. For the Flag Page®, the structural members would be the 23 Soft traits and 23 Hard traits. These scores tell a great deal about how a person succeeds. They are I-beams because they reach deep into the 56 traits when a person scores them and tells them so much about how that person voted and exactly where their core nature lies...Soft, Balancing or Hard.

Then we look at the outside surface of the building. This is the Flag itself. It is the obvious behavior you can observe most frequently. Like the outside of the building, the Top Five Motivations are attractive and represent who the person is at his or her best.

Finally, we look at the crown of the building where all the architectural details come together. In the Flag Page®, this would be the person's Home and Adopted countries. The very first feature seen on the skyline is the building's unique silhouette and the very first thing observable in people is their natural Home country behavior...Control, Fun, Perfect or Peace.

The Ultimate Tool

The Flag Page® is a powerful tool in helping people discover who they are. Now, with one simple and colorful printout, you will have insights you may never had before.

The Four Countries will give you insight into how to expect a person will act and know the type of words and "language" that person will best respond to.

The *hard and soft* scale will let you know how a person will react to your input. If they have a high *soft* score, they will be very relational, but be careful – they will tend to view your input in terms of "friend or foe" and can offend easily. If a person has a high *hard* score they will not likely respond to "warm & fuzzies". They like to view input in terms of "right or wrong" and they generally tend to be less patient and flexible. They prefer that you be very direct and to the point with them. They are driven by results. And the higher the hard score, the more impervious they are to being offended.

The Flag reveals the true heart of an individual. When you learn the definition of each term and they develop their "Rules to Feel Loved" you will have a clear understanding of what that person truly needs out of life.

Finally, the Talents section will give you a summary of where a person will most likely succeed in life by showing you where a person's core interests lie.

One important tool that we provide you with is a computer print out that explains each person and how their Flag Page® can be interpreted. The Flag Page® program takes your input, compares it to everything it knows about the Flag Page® motivations and creates your customized paragraphs on each section: Country, Hard and Soft, the Flag, and Talents.

We recommend you take the time to print out the pages and have someone read the descriptive paragraphs to you. Why not read it yourself? You certainly can if you like, but we have discovered that there is something very powerful and special about hearing it as opposed to seeing it. There is something extremely validating when a person hears someone else say what is right about them. If you are doing the Flag Page® as a couple, we suggest that the husband and wife read the paragraphs to each other.

Keep in mind that this is a computer's interpretation of your Flag Page®. Simply disregard anything you feel is not accurate.

Appendix - The 56 Motivations

When one of the 56 words below shows up in a person's Flag, it takes on a life of its own and affects everything the person is and does. In this high position, the word is no longer just a trait, it is a MOTIVATOR. For this reason, we call the following list, the 56 Motivations.

When you filled out your Flag, you eliminated 51 others in order to pick these particular five as the ones that are most important to you. These five motivations are the key to understanding just who you are and who God made you to be.

ARTISTIC

Definition: *Putting your own personal stamp on making something more attractive is very rewarding for you.*

Observations: People who put Artistic in their Flag get major emotional rewards from creating a visually attractive environment. Unattractive surroundings can stress you out, in fact, just sitting in a plain room with nothing but bare walls can create stress in you. You want to create beauty.

AVOIDS CONFLICT

Definition: *You stay away from troublesome people and avoid arguments.*

Observations: Others can often interpret this love of "avoiding conflict" as a sign that you "just don't care". But nothing could be farther from the truth. You do care. It is just that you so desire to avoid conflict, you will quietly pull away to avoid a fight. Why? Because avoiding conflict helps you to feel safe and secure. Avoiding conflict is not so much about desiring peace. At some level you may understand that conflict is necessary, like when Jesus threw the money changers out of the temple. Actually, avoiding conflict is about protecting yourself. To you, avoiding conflict equals avoiding stress, avoiding pain and avoiding loss.

BOLD

Definition: *You are daring and are willing to accomplish what others wouldn't even imagine.*

Observations: Among the people who place Bold in their Flags, some love it because they feel stronger by doing things that other people are not willing to do. Others choose it because they feel more empowered when they are standing up for what they believe in. Bold gives them that feeling. Visions of risk taking, new directions, and breaking away from the conventions of what others say cannot or should not be done, are all being carried in the word Bold. Bold is about acting even in the face of fear. Bold says, "I refuse to be afraid!" Bold agrees with the Apostle Paul when he said, "I can do all things through Christ who strengthens me."

BORN LEADER

Definition: *You set the pace and direction for others to follow. You lead the way.*

Observations: When Born Leader is chosen, you are saying that you love to take responsibility, call the shots and grab the horns of leadership. In short, you love to be in charge. Emotionally, Born Leader strikes a chord that rings all the right notes in you of taking responsibility, setting the pace, being the one at the front who everyone looks to for what should be done.

Born leaders actually love the fact that most people don't want to be in charge. It makes it easier for you to step to the front and start directing the action. Your biggest challenge can come when you run into someone else who also loves to be in charge, and then the battle is on.

For many born leaders, if you can't call the shots, you would rather not get involved at all. This can bring a lot of criticism. People may accuse you of being an "egotist" or more concerned about being in the lime light than in accomplishing the goal at hand. But this is not the case. For deep inside you is a voice that most never hear. It is a voice that causes you to want to be the one to lead the charge, even though doing so may mean you may be the first one to get shot.

This motivation, however, can cause you to reach for responsibilities when, in fact, you are really not ready, and this can get you into a lot of hot water. This usually affects those who have a strong leadership motivation, but are still young and unproven in their abilities. You need to be aware that leading must be learned and earned. Just having the desire is rarely enough. You need to take the time to prepare.

CALM

Definition: *You like to be relaxed, stress free and are able to put others at ease. You like it when others put you at ease too.*

Observations: Loving Calm so much that it appears in your Flag means that you are seeking an environment free from the stresses of tense relationships, challenging people and sticky circumstances. People who love

Calm know what disturbs their tranquility, and they are intent on avoiding circumstances and avoiding people who tend to rock the boat and cause conflict. The very word Calm itself produces a sensation in you that brings relief, rest, relaxation, a slow pace and the removal of all that is stressful. The people who put this in their Flag are giving everyone a message: Emotional stress is unwelcome here.

CHEERFUL

Definition: *You stay upbeat and pleasant no matter how you might feel inside.*

Observations: Cheerful people are wonderfully pleasant to be around. You are always looking for genuine reasons to be Cheerful, even when few reasons can be found. Those who place this motivation in their Flag are giving a clear message that no matter how you may feel, you will not let anyone know how stressed out you truly are inside. This is a motivation and a belief placed inside of you that says, "Never let them see you sweat". In daily behavior you strive to be upbeat under all conditions.

For some of you, however, cheerful can be a defense mechanism. By staying cheerful, you are able to deflect the attempts of others who may want to get too close. Cheerful can be a pleasant way of saying, "I'm OK, don't come any closer."

COMPETENT

Definition: *You do everything you can to be good at what you do.*

Observations: People who love to be competent get an endorphin rush from the idea that they can produce work, a project, and accomplishment that is beyond criticism and excels in every way. Just the thought that you would be beyond reproach is a safe feeling and also one that gives you the claim, "I'm good enough now".

Indeed, you are good at everything you do. What you don't tell people, is that you only do things you are good at. If you can't be absolutely assured you will succeed at a given task, you simply will not attempt it. This can often frustrate others who do not understand why you don't want to get involved in whatever it is they want you to do. They think, "You're good at everything else, why won't you help me with this?" and then they can take offense. They may even insult you in an attempt to motivate you to do what they ask. You may find it helpful to just be honest with others when they ask you to do something you are not comfortable with. Simply let them know that you don't just "do" things unless you have the time, experience or knowledge to be very proficient in what you do. They still may not like it, but at least you can try to keep them from reading anything overly negative into your hesitancy.

CONSISTENT

Definition: *You like things to stay the same.*

Observations: This is a passionate need for things to stay as they are. Consistency creates a feeling of safety and protection. Sometimes, just the idea of change can cause uncertainty and create feelings of fear and stress in you. Others may criticize you for seeming "inflexible", but it is not that you don't want change. You just want to know where the consistency will be *before* there is a change. Stability is important in life and you have a real sense for stability and the safety it brings. When people check with you before there is change, it gives you the chance to weigh in on the proposed changes before they occur, allowing you to check for needed stability ahead of time. If change is forced on you, even small changes like new staplers can cause you to become very defensive.

CREATIVE

Definition: *You like to solve problems, invent things, and see things differently.*

Observations: To some who put Creative in their Flag it says problem solving. To others it says inventiveness and change for the better. Still to others it can be restricted to the arts, poetry or music, but to all it signals a way to improve their lives and the lives of other people. It causes you to be open to the new and the untested.

It should be noted that creative people really own what they do. Since they are creating, they are always interested in what others think of their creations and solutions. However, what they are looking for is validation, NOT critique. In other words, you don't really want to know what others "think". You desire approval of what you have created, or at the very least, constructive criticism. Creative people seem to always be asking, "What do you think?" But brutal honesty is not what you are looking for, and when others are insensitive and critical, it can be very painful for you. Always encourage other people to temper their critiques with compliments.

CURIOUS

Definition: *You're on a continuous search for information about everything. You want answers.*

Observations: People who have Curious in their Flag are always asking, "WHY?" Your constant quest for answers causes you endless fascination with stories, new information, new people, new situations and new events. You are excited about exploration of places, people and ideas.

Sadly, the lovers of Curious are the first people to be accused of being nosy. Your search for answers to questions like "Who just drove up?", "What's in that box?", and "Who's your new boyfriend?" can easily be misunderstood as prying and inappropriate. But being nosy is not your motive, and you don't mean to pry or be inappropriate. You are simply blessed with an insatiable need to know and to understand. When your grade school teacher said, "There is no such thing as a stupid question" you lit up. You then probably challenged the teacher's patience and caused her to reevaluate the belief that "there is no such thing as a stupid question." To you, the need to know is simply greater than the need for appropriate behavior or proper timing or not asking too many questions. You love to learn and you love to discover. This is what helps to make you the wonderful person you are.

DEEP THINKER

Definition: *You are very good at analyzing and thinking about situations before and after they happen. You look for the reasons why.*

Observations: Oh, how the Deep Thinker can think! When this phrase winds up in your Flag it is because you want to validate your need to quietly and continuously process every event, idea and behavior with questions that confirm or deny the rightness of what is about to happen or analyze what just happened. (Whew - just writing the sentence describing you takes a lot of thinking!) Because you love to analyze, it can be difficult for you to make fast decisions about anything because you need time to process things. Only by truly thinking things through can you feel secure in your decisions. Of course, this desire to "think before you act" can get you into trouble with those who want to move more quickly. It is not unusual for a Deep Thinker to marry someone with Quick to Action in their Flag. You can imagine the interesting discussions this can create! Also, people from Fun Country and Control Country can test the patience of Deep Thinkers. Fun and Control people want to take off *now* and don't seem to mind slamming into walls now and then. Such an idea is inconceivable to the Deep Thinker. "Why hit a wall if you can avoid the wall in the first place?" Even though Deep Thinkers can draw criticism from others, they often save those same people a lot of pain and cost by insisting that they slow down and consider all the options before taking off.

DRY SENSE OF HUMOR

Definition: *You have deep and profound insights that allow you to creatively make comments that are both insightful and funny!*

Observations: If there is one thing you do well, it is to make others laugh when everyone least expects it. People may not understand a clever and surprising comment you make until it sinks in, and then they all laugh. The word "Dry" means that the humor is void of any attempt to be funny for the sake of getting attention. Unlike a person who uses humor to gain attention, it is not attention you crave. Instead, you just want to make a statement of opinion and it is the creative way in which you frame this statement that causes others to see the unexpected humor in your comment.

On the darker side, this dry humor can, at times, become biting and critical when not properly controlled. On the positive side, this talent gives you the ability to break up tense situations and put everyone else at ease with clever and insightful comments.

EASY WAY

Definition: *When there's a choice to make, you favor areas where there are no hassles or problems in your way.*

Observations: While it may seem unrealistic to some, those who love the Easy Way never stop trying to find ways to create a life without obstacles, set backs, failures or frustrations. This comes from the fact that you go above and beyond the call of duty to keep from rocking the boat or contributing to an already tense situation. Loving the Easy Way in this case means loving the path of no resistance. Easy Way people can find themselves being criticized because they are reluctant to get involved or make commitments, but this is not because you don't care. You just want to stay away from situations you feel could become difficult.

EASY GOING

Definition: *You take life as it comes and enjoy having a good time with many different people. You don't want things to rock your world.*

Observations: Maintaining the things the way they are and predictability is the goal for the person who loves the emotions raised by the phrase Easy Going. Much like Easy Way (above), Easy Going expresses the same kind of need. When you see both of these appear in a Flag, it is a major statement. Most often, the "two Easys" show up in the Flags of people from Peace country.

ECONOMICAL

Definition: *You save money whenever possible and you know where almost every dime is spent to avoid waste.*

Observations: A person who puts Economical in his or her Flag has an important need for financial security. You are always searching for ways to save money and to know the status of your financial security. A good nickname for Economical is "personal banker", because that's what you can be like when it comes to managing money. Sometimes you can be unfairly characterized as cheap or stingy. But it is not about being cheap. In fact, it is often not even about money at all -- it's about being secure.

ENTHUSIASTIC

Definition: *You can get behind ideas and people with energy and show everyone how you feel.*

Observations: This trait is all about showing feelings. It's about putting those emotions out where everyone can see them and ultimately approve of them. When you put Enthusiastic in your Flag, you are making a big statement to the world that you are firing on all cylinders and no one should try and force you to keep your opinions to yourself. You simply can't. Your energy can be very inspiring to those around you and can even make others feel safe. They will think, "If he/she can be so enthusiastic, maybe we really can succeed."

FAITHFUL

Definition: *You are loyal and committed to only a few people you really trust. You want those people to be loyal to you.*

Observations: Faithful people can be difficult to get close to. You often build an emotional barbed-wire fence around yourself. If people can get over, they are in for life -- if they die in the attempt to get in, too bad. They will remain outside your closely guarded inner circle.

Another note: Some Faithful people **really** feel strongly about others being faithful in return and can interpret the slightest transgression as a violation of trust. When you kick someone out of the circle, it is really hard for them to get back in. In such cases, you may need help in understanding the benefits of forgiveness and not holding others to too high a standard.

Faithful is considered the most powerful trait in the Flag Page. There are so many deeply held and serious emotions attached to this trait. You can be confident in stating that people who put Faithful in their Flag have strong expectations for themselves and others because of their need for loyalty, commitment and trust. For many, this trait is also attached to their strongly held faith in God.

FLASHY

Definition: *You love glamour, glitter and showmanship.*

Observations: Historically, only 3% of all Flags will have this trait appear. When it does show up, you are definitely making a statement -- you would rather "stand out" than "fit in". You love clothes that cause people to stop and notice you. For men, it might be big belt buckles, cowboy boots or other gear that no one else is wearing. For women, look for lots of make up, piles of shoes and tons of new "outfits". Outward appearances in clothing and gimmicks are not the point. You have found the feelings transmitted by a certain outward appearance continue to bring you a sense of importance and value. In spite of the criticism received for loving this activity or look, you go on, being who you are, celebrating life everyday with the confidence that says, "Hey, world, look at me!"

FUN

Definition: *You look at the lighter side in most everything and laughter is your best medicine.*

Observations: Fun people are often criticized by others who don't place a high value on "fun". It is almost as if they are saying, "I used to be fun too, when I was six, but I grew up!!" Fun people are often criticized for not "growing up" or of being "immature". Truth is, however, you love to live on the fun side of life, and, assuming you don't kill yourself in some fun activity like hang-gliding, you will likely outlive all of your critics. That is because people who laugh are generally much healthier than those who do not, and Fun people love to laugh. You will laugh if something good happens and you will laugh if something bad happens. You will laugh at your own successes and be the first to laugh at your own failures.

GOAL SETTER

Definition: *You focus on a target until you accomplish your goal.*

Observations: Putting Goal Setter in your Flag means you cannot participate in employment, a project or even a family activity if you do not have goals set and clarified. Goals make it possible for you to have direction and even go so far as to give your life real meaning. It becomes the reason you get up every morning and go on even when the current situation has gone far from what you originally planned. For you, life is simply a matter of walking around with one eye closed and the other eye fastened to your rifle scope. In this scope you see what you are most interested in...your goals. If anyone should attempt to interest you in something outside the picture in your "cross hairs", you quickly let them know you are not interested. This can sometimes cause you to come across as rude. But being rude is not your intention, you simply want to stay focused on what is ahead and don't want anything or anybody to cause you to take your eye off the target.

GOOD LISTENER

Definition: *You want to hear what people have to say. People like it when you are interested in them.*

Observations: This is a trait that many people might call a skill, but it is more than a skill to you. You love to listen to what others have to say. You learn by listening. You totally enjoy hearing the comments and stories of other people. You show others how much you care and respect them by listening to what is important to them. Listening allows you to care for others. This, of course, can be frustrating when a person who loves to listen marries a person who doesn't like to talk. Tension can rise when the one who wants to listen pressures the one who doesn't want to talk. You may try explaining why it is important for you to hear from the other person, but the truth is they are not likely to change anymore than you are. It may be best to find other ways to engage people through listening. Perhaps volunteer to be on the phones for a crisis hotline or offer to be a mentor at your church.

GOOD ON STAGE

Definition: *There is no bigger thrill for you than getting the attention of an audience.*

Observations: Whenever you see Good on Stage in a Flag, you can be almost 99% certain that this person literally loves to be up in front...on a stage. The thrill of applause, the rapt attention of an audience listening to your every word and using every available talent is what brings a vast amount of satisfaction and reward to you. Getting the entire room to pay attention to you ignites all kinds of positive desires and needs. This is your way to feel important. While everyone else in the world is terrified to speak in public, you can't wait for your next appearance.

GREAT SENSE OF HUMOR

Definition: *You like whatever is funny, breaks the ice, and keeps people laughing.*

Observations: The people who vote highly for this trait do so because they process almost every idea and fact through a humorous filter. Humor is an emotional reward in itself, even if you are the only one who is laughing at the idea or event. Humor lubricates life and makes it much less tricky and troublesome. Humor is a release from tension and fear. As a result, people like you tend to live longer than your more serious relatives. Humor allows you to deal with an idea, make it real or handle it in a way that does not cause you stress. Humor handled in this way is sure to get criticism from others in family or work settings who take life so very seriously. People like you, and you can have fun at a funeral, which does not always go over very well with certain family members.

IDEALISTIC

Definition: *Your standards of what ought to be, should be and could be are higher than those of most people.*

Observations: The foundational theme to remember with this trait is the word STANDARDS. Idealistic people set standards for others and themselves to follow. You always seem to dwell on and talk about what should be, could be and ought to be. It is standards that must be met in order to reach your high idea of being both right and justified. The challenge, of course, is that we live in a world where the "ideal" does not always triumph. Idealistic people, when faced with a less-than-perfect scenario can quickly turn to thoughts of "why try if it can't be right". Some idealists can even go to extremes when the ideal is not achieved. For example, the minister who thinks a dirty thought and then reasons that he might as well commit adultery since the ideal of a pure mind was not maintained. (See notes on Perfectionist.)

INDEPENDENT

Definition: *Working by yourself makes you feel like you are more in control of your life.*

Observations: Independent is called one of the "leave me alone twins" along with its sister, Self Sufficient. I call you the "rubber band people". You will get close to someone, but then start to panic and pull away. After you have been "left alone", you begin to feel the need for connecting again and the "rubber band" pulls you back. It does not take long before you pull away again. This, of course, can drive a spouse or co-workers a bit crazy. The best thing they can do, however, is to leave you alone and let the "rubber band" pull you back. Moving towards you with, "Why won't you spend time with me?", is the wrong move. They should let the tension build -- it is what always brings you back to them.

People who choose to love Independent are usually in deep need to stay away from pain at most any cost. Independent is a strong motivator that creates a work ethic that drives success in almost any endeavor. Great sales people and those who own and run companies typically have a love of Independent. People who love this trait need to do as much on their own as possible.

INSPIRATIONAL

Definition: *You need to search out ways to make a difference in the lives of other people.*

Observations: Making a positive impact in someone's life brings new meaning to those who love to be Inspirational. You desire to make a difference, impact lives and do something worthwhile.

While Inspirational can seem like an immeasurable, ethereal concept to others, it is not to you. In fact, you are constantly measuring, "Am I making a difference". Those closest to you must know that it is vitally important for them to give you measured feedback. They need to let you know that you are making a difference. Something like, "My life is better because you did _____" is the kind of emotional feedback that Inspirational people, like you, so desperately crave.

LIFE OF THE PARTY

Definition: *Being in the spotlight and providing a good time for everyone else makes life more fun.*

Observations: Life of the Party creates an open and obvious search for a feeling of importance. In this case, the importance comes in the form of a trade: You come to the party, laugh at my jokes, be a good audience for me and in return, I will make sure you have a great time that you won't soon forget. In this sense, the party will die without the "life" to keep it going. You see yourself as the spark, the key, the engine that keeps social events running in top condition. As one might expect, you have massive social time needs, both on and off the job.

LOW KEY

Definition: *You don't make demands on anybody and don't like making a big deal about things.*

Observations: The people who choose Low Key most often hail from the home country of Peace. What you are saying to the world around you is that you must stay out of the spot light. The twin sister of Low Key is Stay In The Background. These traits bring you a safe passage through difficult situations and life in general. You make the best support person for leaders of any persuasion.

Low Key helps you stay under the radar of people looking for trouble. You love the very sound of the phrase "Low Key" because it indicates a feeling of staying out of harm's way. Also see Easy Going and Easy Way to see how all of these protect their owners from conflict, hassles and demands. You are often the easiest and least demanding person on earth to be with.

LOVES PEOPLE

Definition: *You enjoy being around people and accept everybody without judging them.*

Observations: Why do people who put Loves People in their Flag put it there? Seems obvious...they LOVE people. Don't let the word love throw you off. The word love in context with this Flag choice is not about life long commitment, but rather about bringing more people into your large world of acceptance. You are not prejudiced toward anyone, but are an "includer". You truly find a great sense of joy and fulfillment from being with others.

Sometimes, your can find your spouse feels jealous or threatened by your constant need to be with others. They may feel, "Why can't you just be with me? Aren't I good enough? Why do we always have to be around other people?" It is important that he/she realizes that your need for others is in no way a negative statement towards him/her. You truly need interaction with others to feel fulfilled. It is unlikely that any one individual could meet all of your social needs.

MOVES QUICK TO ACTION

Definition: *When you come up with a good idea you are the first one to get started on it and want others to get on it as well.*

Observations: This trait is the very opposite of Deep Thinker. A Moves Quick person is not about analyzing every little detail, instead you are about taking action right away because this fast action has always paid off for you in the past. You need activity and motion in your life to feel that you are alive, contributing and worthwhile. Your pace can weary other people who don't understand that Moves Quick people are fulfilling a need for accomplishment and the resulting feeling of worth. Should those accomplishments disappear, you can be in danger of various levels of depression.

MUSICAL

Definition: *You love music because of the way it makes you feel.*

Observations: This is very much either a choice made because of skill or simply due to a great interest in music because it "heals the soul". History with people who put Musical in their Flag proves that music is like a medicine. A key word is rhythm. Adding to skill and love of listening, you can also crave a rhythm, an even flow and routine to your life that can become upset if things become highly unpredictable.

NEAT

Definition: *You want your world to be clean, tidy and in order.*

Observations: Putting Neat in your Flag shows that you have a real need for an orderly environment. To you, it equals personal fulfillment. Chaos or messes can stress you out in a big way because to you, neatness is not just a physical condition; it is an emotional state of mind that comes from your environment. As can be expected, your love of Neat can cause you to have enemies who unknowingly step on your emotional need by simply leaving opened cans on counters, pillows on floors or rooms in complete disarray. These can become dramatic insults to you. You can feel as though you are in a never-ending war with those who do not view "neatness" as a high priority. Others can criticize you as "anal" or "compulsive", but these characterizations are unfair. If you love to be Neat, it would be best to explain to those around you that you don't mean to nit-pick or be condemning. It is just that neatness helps to reduce stress in your life so that you can be your best.

When this trait joins together with Organized in a Flag, the two become the Batman and Robin of order, systems and structure. You will have extraordinary talent for putting processes together and making them work without a hitch.

NEVER A DULL MOMENT

Definition: *You need to have something going on all the time. You love being busy.*

Observations: This is the cousin of Moves Quick to Action (see previous). These two traits have much in common because the lovers of these traits have the emotion for motion. The busier you are, the more you feel worthwhile and fulfilled. When Never a Dull Moment and Moves Quick to Action join up in a Flag, you are likely to experience some extremes of over commitment and high involvement in projects and in the lives of other people. Never a Dull Moment brings you a certain kind of joy in activity. The constant series of events does not have to be toward any definite purpose, but can be simply driven by responding and joining into anything that's going on, just as long as "something's happening". Busyness satisfies and causes you to feel complete.

OPTIMISTIC

Definition: *You see the potential in everything and believe there is no limit to what might be possible.*

Observations: Those with Optimistic in their Flag encounter a situation and ask, "How could this work?" This passion for Optimism gives you the ability to chase what you believe in long after everybody else has lost interest. Such a positive trait as Optimistic comes with one classic down side…tunnel vision. Optimistic can put you in such need to reach the better, more promising place, that you find it easy to avoid many other facts. Being Optimistic allows you to stay away from "failing" thinking and focus on what can work rather than what won't work. You are a "glass half full person" and at constant odds with those who seem proud of being able to see that the light at the end of the tunnel is actually a train.

ORGANIZED

Definition: *You have a certain way you want things to be and you work to put order, a system or structure into those things you're interested in.*

Observations: With a passion for organization, systems and structure, you love Organized and have a natural way with the flow of things. You make quick work of filing systems, know the best mail merge program to save money and can tell anyone why a process they have been working with for weeks can be improved with only a few adjustments. You seem to know exactly what the adjustments should be and why you should make them. You are the kind of person who writes books on time management, getting your life together and five tips for more orderly closets. A major emotional need is met for you in your love for Organized. When a situation has a process, a club has a structure, a business has a brochure or the forks are simply put away with other forks, you are having a deep need met that is both fulfilling for you and productive for the people around you. Organized to you means you iron and fold your underwear, have your socks sorted by style and color and virtually every drawer in your house is neat and tidy. The only time you get in trouble is when your need for order becomes a compulsion that drives others crazy. (Of course, to people who are slobs, any amount of organization seems compulsive.) Your love of Organized is your way of putting order into your life.

PATIENT

Definition: *You accept people and are able to forgive their mistakes. You love to be thoughtful and understanding of others.*

Observations: This trait is about the ability to endure. Patient people love the act of waiting for others to act. You are accepting and even enduring of the difficult ways of other people. For you, there is a reward in being there in the background for that moment when you will be needed. You enjoy accepting and sometimes showing great tolerance for people who are not like you. You are the person with the long fuse that rarely sets off the bomb because you keep putting out the fuse.

PEACEFUL

Definition: *You love it when everyone in your life is being calm, relaxed and adaptable.*

Observations: Staying in an acceptable and cooperative state is absolutely essential to you. When people say they want "world peace", they are speaking your language. When conflict breaks out, you either hide until the battle is over or become the ambassador of the world and attempt to mediate. Even if others do not cooperate, you never give up in your effort to create this condition in any way you can. Peaceful takes place when everyone gets along, sees eye to eye and looks for ways to cooperate with one another. Anything or anyone who might threaten Peace can quickly become the enemy. Your solution? Simply stay away and uninvolved and maintain your own personal peace. This is the reason why you can get quiet when someone demands an answer or attempts to dialogue in a raised tone of voice.

PERFECTIONIST

Definition: *You like to fuss over the smallest detail. You know how things should be and you take the time to make it so.*

Observations: Perfectionists tend to be the most brilliant and creative people on earth. Nothing is more fulfilling to you than to have every single facet of a situation line up with your vision of Perfect. This trait is not so much a condition that you arrive at, but rather the act of pursuing Perfection can be the reward itself. It's as if the chase is more rewarding than the result. In an emotionally healthy individual, it causes them to constantly strive for a high level of excellence.

In an emotionally unhealthy person, this striving for perfection can literally drive them nuts. Frustrated perfectionists are in a constant state of war with the world about them and even themselves. Unchecked, frustrated perfectionists can become plagued by a series of physical and emotional ailments. The challenge is for you to be able to strive for excellence while understanding that few things in life are truly "perfect".

PERSISTENT

Definition: *You are driven to get what you want and don't give up until you get it.*

Observations: When Persistent arrives in your Flag, it tells you that there is no mission or purpose in life where you will easily or quickly give up. If there are obstacles in the way of a desire or a need, you step up to the plate and show the world that nothing will stand in your way. This is especially true when the goal you are chasing is a deeply held emotional need such as a cause or greater purpose. A love of Persistent is a love of determination, commitment and following through. Persistent is admired by almost everyone, unless Persistent gets out of hand and appears to be pushy, obnoxious and abrasive, and then this can quickly offend.

PRECISE

Definition: *You like to do things right the first time and that means paying attention to exact details.*

Observations: The people with Precise in their Flag have the talent to build ships in bottles, tamper with scientific instruments and figure out long and difficult equations. This motivation allows you to stay with what is complex, complicated and in need of an exact solution. In effect, when it comes to jobs of dealing with details, you can be a very patient person and the tiniest detail is not missed. Your love of Precise means that nothing will happen fast because Precise takes time. If you are not allowed to take the time you believe is necessary to apply your gift of precision, you ultimately will rebel against the person or situation that is hindering your motivation. Precision and time go hand in hand.

SELF SUFFICIENT

Definition: *You don't need to rely on anyone because you like the freedom of taking your own path.*

Observation: When the Self Sufficient need arrives in your top five, it becomes possible for you to get a great deal of work done without waiting or depending on other people. The love of this motivation allows you to develop your own opinions, act on your own intuition and decide to do what you believe, rather than what the crowd is doing at the time. See "Independent".

SENSITIVE

Definition: *You can pick up people's true feelings and know what they mean without them having to say a word. You feel things very deeply.*

Observations: Sensitive can create a high ability to tune into the needs and feelings of other people to the point that you can interpret entire messages from a single look or a change in voice inflection. This is possible because you love to be in tune with the emotional condition of other people and have had years to practice what you love. I call Sensitive people "emotional reflectors". Treat a Sensitive person with kindness and respect and they will reflect it right back to you -- in fact, they will amplify it. But treat them harshly, and they will also give it right back!

SERIOUS

Definition: *You see life as a series of important issues that must be dealt with in a serious manner. You don't like it when people take things too lightly.*

Observations: People who have Serious in their Flag tend to take life, well...seriously. You have a need to stay away from laughter, jokes, silliness and those that appear to be shallow. You are focused on paying attention to the serious reality of what is happening now, which causes you to stay focused on the task at hand. Because of this motivation, you can often struggle with the requirements of social politeness. You often don't get or understand people's jokes and have not worked your smile muscles for a long time. To Fun people, Serious can seem like a disease that must be cured. But to you, being so makes you feel good, valuable and important.

SINCERE AT HEART

Definition: *You work hard at trying to treat everyone fairly. You like real and genuine people.*

Observations: Sincere at Heart is about two very important ideas: Genuine and Fair. This is one of the most popular motivations that show up in over 50% of all Flags. The first part to understand is that you need to be real. You hate phonies and can spot them across the room. You need real people and want to always to be real yourself. Your second mission is fairness. Sincere at Heart people like you, make fairness almost a religion where you will fight for other people who are not getting fair treatment. You use this as a filtering device to check new people who come into your life, as well as those you already know and trust. Are you for real? Are you fair?

STAY IN THE BACKGROUND

Definition: *You're at your best when you are in a supportive roll, and not the leader.*

Observations: When you Stay in the Background, you have a desire to help others succeed. You see the bigger picture. This is not about "me"; this is about the greater good. Stay in the Background people love to support, stand with and encourage others. If someone else needs you, you are quick to step forward and help -- as long as you won't have to be the one in charge. You are a person who does not crave the spotlight. You seek anonymity. When you see the people or projects you supported succeed and get praise, you light up as well. You know you had a part in making things work and you don't need to get the credit.

STEADY

Definition: *You like things to be predictable, productive and stable.*

Observations: The people who treasure Steady do it because they need a routine in life. Match this word up with Consistent and see how the two create a burning desire for life to stay intact with no surprises, especially surprises that are unpleasant. The phrase "steady as she goes" makes you feel warm all over. The word itself can make you feel more secure. Without exception, people that place Steady in their Flag have been raised by a mother or father who was steady as a rock. That requirement to be steady and dependable was simply duplicated in your life. Disruptive changes and turmoil are your enemy. You desire a predictable life. This, of course, can be a challenge since life is so unpredictable. People may accuse you of being against change, but this is not necessarily true. You can easily change as long as the change is, well... steady.

STRONG WILLED

Definition: *No matter what anyone else thinks, your mind is made up and you'll act on that no matter what.*

Observations: Strong Willed people have inside them an intention that is deliberate. You have no intention of putting the brakes on for the feelings of other people. Your strong will makes it possible for you to accomplish things, push through obstacles and do what you were born to do. You have strong opinions. While this can be interpreted as a negative trait by others, it most certainly is not. You know who you are and what you believe in. You are not easily pushed around by others. Just seeing a clever ad on TV does not make you run out and say, "Oooo, I just have to have that!" You will not surrender when things don't go your way. You are the one who perseveres in the face of opposition and conflict. The good news is that when you are right, no one can talk you out of doing the right thing. The bad news is that when you are wrong, it is virtually impossible for you to see it until you fail.

SYMPATHETIC

Definition: *You feel what others are feeling. You are responsive, agreeable and understanding to the needs of others.*

Observations: Sympathetic people are amazing in their ability to feel what others feel. You can understand, relate to and feel compassion for the plight of other people. You offer a gift of acceptance that is difficult to find in this world. You are virtually identical to someone who is Sensitive. Combine both Sympathetic and Sensitive on the same Flag and you are a person who can truly reflect the feelings of others.

See "Sensitive".

THOUGHTFUL

Definition: *You are considerate and caring of the needs of other people.*

Observations: You are a Thoughtful person who needs to serve other people and think of their needs, often instead of your own. Your ability to reach out and think of ways to serve others before even learning what those needs are is an astounding thing to see. It comes with no real effort on your part. Thoughtful pours out of you like a spring and seems to shut off only in the most challenging of circumstances. If you have Thoughtful in your Flag, you most likely will have many other "people loving" traits as well.

THRIVES ON ENCOURAGEMENT

Definition: *You love it when people build you up and believe in you.*

Observations: People who Thrive on Encouragement do literally that; they thrive. If people give you Encouragement, you come alive like a flower does to sunshine and rain. Others can tell you how incredibly wonderful you are ten times a day and it is never too much. People are often hesitant to give you what you so desperately need, fearing that too much encouragement may lead to overly elevated levels of self-esteem and too big of a head. But nothing could be farther from the truth. This is not about "ego" to you, this is about being validated.

Thrives on Encouragement can be an Achilles' heel for you if you have a Flag that is very strong -- Fun, Bold, Self Sufficient, Born Leader, etc. Everything about you seems to communicate, "I don't need to be encouraged", when in fact your need for it is deep and profound. It is important that the people closest to you, particularly your spouse, recognize and meet this vital need.

TONS OF CONFIDENCE

Definition: *You are self-assured and have no doubt on the best course of action.*

Observations: This is a trait from the Leading talent family and says "I can do it!" People who quickly identify with Tons of Confidence come in two varieties. The first is the person who has real confidence and rarely shirks back from any new challenge or opportunity because your great ability carries you through. The other is a person who wishes to be confident so much and so often, that any opportunity to identify with confidence is taken, even if you are deeply insecure but trying way too hard to be someone you are not yet. If you are like this, you will need a great deal of patience until you obtain the skills you will need so you can become the confident person you were destined to be.

UNEMOTIONAL

Definition: *You are stable and consistent and don't care for the emotional ups and downs of others.*

Observations: When someone chooses to put Unemotional in their Flag, it is a rare event indeed -- not many people do it. The choice of placing this motivation in the Flag is in reaction to emotional people. You are saying that in your history you have a learned contempt for people who are unpredictable. If someone says to you, "You don't really care for unpredictable people do you?" You will give a hearty agreement. You have disrespect for those who cannot control their feelings. You are proud of the fact that you are not overly emotional. Your challenge is that others can perceive you to be overly cold.

UNIQUE

Definition: *You don't like to follow the crowd. You enjoy being different. You march to the beat of a different drummer.*

Observations: Whenever you put Unique in your Flag, you are saying that you are a person who goes left when everyone else goes right. You march to your own drummer and actually work at being different than the people around you. You are a person who secretly searches for ways to be different in dress, opinion, choices and any other way you can put your unique stamp on the world. Is everyone wearing a team jacket? You deliberately won't own one. Everyone taking the train, you take the bus. This constant pursuit of the alternative life is richly rewarding and fulfilling with each Unique event and expression you are able to create. Most frustrating to you is being in a job where you cannot contribute your special way of doing things because some standardized way is required. As a Unique person, you could probably not work in a franchise where everything must be done according to the manual.

WARM

Definition: *You are friendly, easy to approach and people find it easy to get close to you.*

Observations: Warm people like you are approachable because your great love is connecting with other people. Anything that divides or separates you from others makes life more difficult. The old telephone company slogan "reach out and touch someone" was probably created by a person with Warm in their Flag.

WATCH PEOPLE

Definition: *You notice the little things about people. You enjoy watching others and learning how they do what they do.*

Observations: For you who highly prizes Watch People, actively seeking out situations where people can be found is your priority. But this is to watch, not necessarily to get involved. This is why you make an excellent supporter of those who lead.

You might remember those ads promoting life in the Navy with a technician sitting in a dark room aboard a ship and staring at a radar screen that is scanning the area for movement. This is what you are doing with your talent. Watching People is how you learn about them, as well as how you entertain yourself. People and their ways are an endless source of fascination for you.

WITTY

Definition: *You're clever and unexpected in the jokes you make. You take things that other people think are serious and find the humor in it.*

Observations: You can be depended on to come up with those ice breaker comments to loosen everyone up. Clever, comic, and sometimes sarcastic, you have the gift of unconventional entertainment. This kind of humor makes you clever in your insights about human nature. Some of the best comedians have Witty in their Flags. It is the engine that produces their material.

.

Notes

Chapter 2
1. Florence Littauer, Your Personality Tree (Word Publishing, 1986), p. 22.

Chapter 5
1. Kevin Leman, The Birth Order Book (Fleming H. Revell, 1998), p. 115.

Chapter 8
1. Randy Alcorn, The Grace and Truth Paradox: Responding with Christlike Balance (Multnomah, 2003), p. 16-17.

Pastor Mark and Debbie Gungor

Mark Gungor is the CEO of Laugh Your Way America and Senior Pastor of Celebration Church. Married to Debbie for 36 years and counting, he is also the creator of the highly regarded Laugh Your Way to a Better Marriage* seminar.

Mark believes that the key to a successful marriage is not about finding the right person; it's about doing the right things. If you do the right things you will succeed, if you don't, you'll fail. It's just that simple. Our goal is to help couples get along, get it right, have fun and achieve a successful marriage. Laugh Your Way America exists to eliminate divorce in America, one family at a time.

Laugh Your Way America!, LLC
3475 Humboldt Road
Green Bay, WI 54311
866-52-LAUGH
www.laughyourway.com

THE FLAG PAGE SOLUTION

Now that you've discovered your child's heart, it's time you discover the great things God has in store for you by creating your own Flag Page. The Flag Page is an incredible on-line program designed to help you discover who you are, what you love the most about life and most importantly…who God created you to be.

The entire assessment takes 10 minutes and is great for teens, parents, grandparents, co-workers… the list goes on and on. To get started, log onto www.flagpage.com. It's inexpensive, easy and life-changing.

DISCOVERING YOUR HEART WITH THE FLAG PAGE

In his book Discovering Your Heart with the Flag Page, national marriage speaker Mark Gungor explains how to interpret and understand the colorful printout that is the Flag Page. He shows the reader how to understand why they act and react the way they do, and what important needs they have in their life that are the keys to their success and happiness.

Order your copy at www.laughyourway.com

www.flagpage.com

LAUGH YOUR WAY TO A BETTER MARRIAGE

For the first time ever, the entire life-changing Laugh Your Way to a Better Marriage Event is available on DVD!

Filmed in Phoenix, Arizona, this 4-Disc DVD set includes every minute of Mark Gungor's weekend seminar, as well as an extra DVD featuring Mark answering the questions he couldn't cover during the original taping. With over 6 hours of material, the DVD set captures all the fun and facts of Mark's look at life, love, and marriage. Mark will walk you through from beginning to end as you laugh, learn and realize you can make immediate positive change in your own marriage. Perfect for couples, singles and youth, this set makes a great gift. From "The Tale of Two Brains" to the funny, hard-hitting, and must-hear information in "The Number One Key to Incredible Sex", Mark will have you laughing your way to a better marriage in no time!

SEX, DATING & RELATING - TEEN EDITION

As Mark travels the country speaking on the subject of marriage, many have said, "I wish I'd known this when I was younger. Do you have this information for my kids or grandkids?"

Here is the highly anticipated and much sought after information on dating and sex that we all wish we had known growing up. In the society and culture we live in today, it is more important than ever that parents and teens are armed with the real facts and the truth. It's time to cut through all the nonsense that is taught in the media, the education system and even the Church.

Together, Mark and Pam Stenzel bring parents and teens the hard-hitting, no-nonsense wisdom not often heard in the secular or faith culture today. Messages that will help teens and their families make wise decisions enabling the next generation to build strong and successful marriages and families…without all the physical and emotional baggage.

These and many more resources are all available at www.laughyourway.com

Listen to the Mark Gungor Show LIVE Monday - Friday from 10:00am - 11:00am Central Time. Join Mark as he discusses any and all issues concerning live, love and marriage.

www.markgungorshow.com